DAY-TO-DAY
BUSINESS
ACCOUNTING

Books in the "Run Your Own Business" Series

Choosing a Legal Structure for Your Business
0-13-603366-0

Computerizing Your Business
0-13-603374-1

Day-to-Day Business Accounting
0-13-603358-X

Financing Your Business
0-13-603382-2

Managing Your Employees
0-13-603341-5

Promoting Your Business with Free (or Almost Free) Publicity
0-13-603390-3

Day-to-Day Business Accounting

Arlene K. Mose, CPA

John Jackson, CPA

Gary Downs, CPA

Prentice Hall
Englewood Cliffs, New Jersey 07632

Library of Congress Cataloging-in-Publication Data

Mose, Arlene K.
  Day-to-day business accounting / Arlene K. Mose, John Jackson,
Gary Downs.
    p.   cm.
    ISBN 0-13-603358-X
    1. Accounting.   2. Managerial accounting.   3. Business
enterprises—Taxation.   I. Jackson, John.   II. Downs, Gary.
III. Title.
HF5635.J186   1997
657—dc21   96-39733
                                                                CIP

Printed in the United States of America

Printing 10   9   8   7   6   5   4   3   2   1

ATTENTION: CORPORATIONS AND SCHOOLS

Prentice Hall books are available at quantity discounts with bulk purchase for educational, business, or sales promotional use. For information, please write to: Prentice Hall Career & Personal Development Special Sales, 113 Sylvan Avenue, Englewood Cliffs, NJ 07632. Please supply title of book, ISBN number, quantity, how the book will be used, date needed.

PRENTICE HALL
Career & Personal Development
Englewood Cliffs, NJ 07632
A Simon & Schuster Company

ISBN 0-13-603358-X

Prentice-Hall International (UK) Limited, *London*
Prentice-Hall of Australia Pty. Limited, *Sydney*
Prentice-Hall Canada, Inc., *Toronto*
Prentice-Hall Hispanoamericana, S.A., *Mexico*
Prentice-Hall of India Private Limited, *New Delhi*
Prentice-Hall of Japan, Inc., *Tokyo*
Simon & Schuster Asia Pte. Ltd., *Singapore*
Editora Prentice-Hall do Brasil, Ltda., *Rio de Janeiro*

Contents

6 The Joys of Hiring Employees   *79*

7 Employee vs. Independent Contractor   *91*

8 **Taxes** *109*

9 **Insurance** *125*

Preface: Beyond Long Division

The preface of any book usually divulges the reasoning or approach the authors used in drafting their *masterpiece.* In our particular case, the initial reasoning appeared unduly simplified. First, we were asked to write a book. Second, we were asked in November when tax accountants have nothing to do anyway.

There is, however, a more involved reason behind our decision to become authors.

Much of the book was already in a draft format as a response to the recurrent questions of our new business clients. It seemed that everyone asked those same *"what about ...?"* questions over and over again. We couldn't help but notice that many clients did not understand the basic concepts of accounting. Every tax season, one of our older clients awes over our handiwork. *"I am so impressed, "* she praises. *"I just never was any good at math!"* It took us a while to realize that she was talking about our accounting. She was not making the distinction between two very different theories of study.

Mathematics is the science of studying the relationships between quantities as represented by numbers. Accounting, on the other hand, is the system of recording and summarizing business and financial transactions and analyzing, verifying, and reporting the results. The accountants merely use numbers to record, summarize, analyze, verify and report. Accounting is a theory of accountability beyond the math function of adding and subtracting. It is way beyond long division. Of course, the reason they are often confused is because both mathematicians and accountants look like nerdy little gnomes, devoid of personality, who are extremely intelligent and have codfish eyes.

It wasn't until we actually tried to explain this strange accounting theory in Chapters 3 and 4 and 5 that we realized why it often takes four years of college study (if not more). Don't be concerned if it takes you more than one reading to grasp the concepts. We made every effort to maintain the text in a form that would be manageable by those who are not acquainted with the theories of business accounting. Although this may be perceived as a "how-to book," the real purpose is to create a broader knowledge and understanding which will help guard you against mistakes made by lack of awareness. Let's face it, there can be no hope for successfully running your small business if the accounting and tax issues do not even come to light.

Regardless of what we have painstakingly tried to explain, there is even more that we have left out. This book cannot supply all the answers to the accounting issues that may arise in your specific business. Although we have made references to other authorities, books, and publications, this printing is obviously not a collection of all of the relevant authorities on the subject of tax or accounting. With some study and self-education, it is possible that you can gain an awareness and general understanding of the significant issues which will assist you in running your business. However, keep these words in mind: *"the devil is in the details."* It is the intricacy of the accounting issues that invariably create the problems of how to record, summarize, analyze, verify, and report.

The concept of a business team cannot be overemphasized. You should make sure that your accounting efforts are supplemented with some input or advice from a trained professional. Our experience has shown us that money spent up front for sound financial and legal advice is always cheaper than the many thousands it takes to correct a legal mess or accounting nightmare. The most successful businesses are those that develop and make use of a good business team to include an attorney, CPA, and financial planner.

Shortly into the writing of this book, our co-author, John, lost his twenty-one-year-old son, Mike. This book is dedicated to the spirit of his youth. It is also dedicated to our respective partners and families for the unquestioning love and support they give us—tax season, after tax season, after tax season. It is because of them that we retain our sanity, remain grounded, meet our publishing deadlines, and avoid disappearing between the lines of some vast intricate ledger sheet.

We couldn't do it without them. And besides, we fish-eyed nerds need the honesty of a loved one who will tell us when our clothes don't match.

Best of luck with your new business venture.

AKM
GPD
JDJ

1

Selecting the Legal Entity for Your Business

One of the first major decisions you will have to make as you start your new business is selecting the type of legal entity. To a large degree, this decision may be dictated by the way you have organized your operations and whether you intend to work on your own or in conjunction with others.

The form of entity you choose can have a significant impact on the way you are protected under the law and the way you are affected by income tax rules and regulations. There are a variety of forms of business organizations. Each has its own benefits and drawbacks and each is treated differently for legal and tax purposes.

Regardless of your choice of legal entity, you should seek the advice of competent legal counsel and business-oriented accountants. You may also want to refer to the book entitled *Choosing a Legal Structure for Your Business* by Stuart A. Handmaker, also in the *Run Your Own Business* series.

SOLE PROPRIETORSHIP

A sole proprietorship is typically a business owned and operated by one individual, or very often by a husband and wife. It is not considered to be a separate legal entity under the law, but rather is an extension of the individual who owns it. The owner has possession of the business assets and is directly responsible for the debts and other liabilities incurred by the business.

This is perhaps the easiest form of business to own and operate because it does not require any specific legal organization, except of course, the normal requirements such as licenses or permits. A sole proprietorship typically does not have any rules or operating regulations under which it must function. The business decisions are solely the result of the owner's abilities.

A sole proprietorship is considered to be a component of the individual's personal tax situation. Individuals operating as sole proprietorships should be aware that their tax liability is contingent on their business income. Tax planning and estimated payments will need to be made as discussed in Chapter 8. When your file your annual tax return in April, you will need to include a separate form called a *Schedule C* which reports the income and expenses related to your business. A copy of a Schedule C is shown at the end of Chapter 8. The Schedule C is NOT included in the IRS booklet which is mailed out at tax time. You will need to make a separate trip to the IRS office or hire a trained professional to assist you with your return.

In addition to this Schedule C, if your business has net income, then a *Schedule SE* must be prepared to determine the amount of social security and FICA taxes you must pay. This is often referred to as the self-employment tax. A Schedule SE is also shown at the end of Chapter 8.

PARTNERSHIPS

Partnerships can take two legal forms: **general** or **limited.** In a general partnership, two or more individuals join together to run the business enterprise. Each of the individual partners has an ownership interest in the company assets and personal responsibility for liabilities, as well as authority in running the business. The authority of the partners, and the way in which profits or losses are to be shared, can be modified by the partnership agreement. The responsibility for liabilities can also be modified by agreement among the partners, but **partnership creditors typically have recourse to the personal assets of each of the partners individually** for settlement of partnership debts. This means if the partnership cannot pay its bills, the creditors will go to the individual partner with the deepest pockets.

A partnership is not a taxable entity. It is treated as a "conduit" through which taxable income is passed to the individual partners for inclusion in their respective tax returns. **A partnership is governed by very complex partnership tax rules** under Subchapter K of the Internal Revenue Code. Partnerships are required to file Federal Form 1065 and generally a state equivalent such as California Form 565. No tax is due with these forms. However, these returns do include a Schedule K-1 which lists the various items of income, expense, and credits to be included on the individual partners' tax return. Just as the sole proprietor pays taxes on "net income," each partner must be aware of her/his share of partnership income to appropriately calculate "income tax," "self-employment tax," and make adequate estimated tax payments.

A **limited partnership** is comprised of one or more general partners who are personally liable for partnership debts, and one or more limited partners who contribute capital and share in the profits or loss of the business. Limited partners are limited as to the liability they have for debts. Limited partners may jeopardize their "limited liability" by participating in the control of the business. As a result, they should not take part in running the business; they may be held liable for the debts of the partnership.

The rights, responsibilities and obligations of both the limited and general partners are typically detailed in the partnership agreement. It is a good idea to have a written, well thought out agreement for any type of partnership. In almost all situations, the legal fees and grief necessary to dissolve the "handshake agreement" are many times greater than the costs and efforts of obtaining a good document in the first place.

Some states will assess an additional tax ANNUALLY on limited partnerships. This tax is paid for the privilege of doing business in the state as a "limited partnership." It is not related to any amount of income or gain which you may have.

C-CORPORATION

A corporation is a separate legal entity which exists under the authority granted by the Secretary of State. A corporation has its own legal rights, is responsible for its own debts, and pays its own taxes. Corporate income does not flow through to the individual. Typically, the owners or stockholders are protected from the liabilities of the business. However, when a corporation is small, creditors often require personal guarantees of the principal owners before extending credit. The legal protection afforded the owners of a corporation can far outweigh the additional expense of starting and administering a corporation.

Incorporation of a business allows a number of other advantages, such as the ease of bringing in additional capital through the sale of stock, or the flexibility of allowing shareholders to sell or transfer their interest in the company. It also provides for business continuity when the original owners choose to retire or sell their interest.

There is a state filing fee to "reserve" a corporate name. A corporation must also adopt and file Articles of Incorporation and Bylaws which govern the rights and obligations of the stockholders, directors and officers (an additional filing fee). You should check with your Secretary of State about any additional assessments for the "privilege" of doing business as a corporation. A corporation is also responsible for holding annual meetings and documenting all policy decisions in the corporate minutes.

A corporation must file annual federal income tax returns with the Internal Revenue Service using Form 1120. A state return must also be filed with the state tax board of any state in which the corporation is doing business.

There are many special accounting elections made in the corporation's first tax return such as year end, method of accounting, and the set up of "organizational" expenses. **They can have a significant impact on how your business will be taxed in future years.**

S-CORPORATION

An S-Corporation is a type of corporation that has special treatment under the tax laws. Basically it is a corporation in all aspects, except that it is not taxed at the corporate level. An S-Corporation usually starts as a C-Corporation and then receives a special recognition from the IRS. This recognition is granted after an IRS review. Even if you have paid an attorney to incorporate you and your corporation records indicate that you are and S-Corporation, the S status is not necessarily official. It must be approved by the IRS.

The government taxes this type of entity in a manner similar to that of a partnership, i.e., the various items of income, expense, and credits flow through to the individual stockholders and are taxed at the "individual" level rather than at the "corporate" level. **Income and losses must be allocated among the shareholders based on stock ownership percentage. Distributions to shareholders must be based on the stock ownership percentages.**

An S-Corporation cannot have more than 35 shareholders and may have only one class of stock. There are additional restrictions and requirements regarding S-Corporate issues. Keep in mind that failure to satisfy S-Corporate requirements result in the loss of eligibility and a reversion to "C-Corporation." The required tax forms for an S-Corporation include the Federal Form 1102-S and state forms such as the California Form 100S. Some states also tax the corporate income before it flows through to the individual shareholder.

LIMITED LIABILITY COMPANY (LLC)

Limited liability companies (LLCs) are hybrid business entities created by statute which combine certain characteristics of corporations with other characteristics associated with partnerships. LLCs are intended to provide limited liability to its owners, have the ability to hold property in its own name, and sue or be sued (similar to a corporation). LLCs, like partnerships, offer the advantages of one level of tax without the restrictions of an S-Corporation. LLCs permit non-pro rata distributions and special allocations of profits and losses.

For various political reasons, licensed professional practices cannot use LLCs in most states. Some states have authorized a variation of the general partnership called "Limited Liability Partnership" or "Registered Limited Partnership" to be used by licensed professionals. In general, these entities relieve a general partner from the liabilities associated with the negligence or wrongful acts of his partners. The general partner still remains liable for his/her own harmful acts and wrong doing and is also still liable for the general contractual liabilities of the entity itself (except for non-recourse debt).

There are many advantages and disadvantages to being an LLC and each factor should be weighed carefully before choosing this type of legal entity.

Don't feel bad if you feel overwhelmed with all the information and decisions. Some accounting books will try to tell you that setting up legal entities and accounting systems is easy. It's a good idea so do some research and more reading. You may even consider an hour or two of consulting time from an attorney or Certified Public Accountant before you make an irreversible decision.

WHY CHOOSE A CPA?

Many people mistakenly consider bookkeeping and accounting to be one in the same.

Bookkeeping is the systematic recording of business transactions in financial terms. Usually the study of bookkeeping emphasizes technique, while the study of accounting emphasizes theory. Although accounting does include the recording of economic events, it goes a step further by carefully identifying, measuring, and communicating these results. A certified public accountant (CPA) offers expert services to the general public in the same way a doctor or lawyer does. CPAs must fulfill certain education requirements which usually means a college degree and certain experience requirements like that of an internship. In addition, a CPA must pass a rigorous three-day examination as well as an ethics exam. Most CPAs are also subject to quality control standards. It is the only profession which monitors and regulates itself by requiring each CPA firm to have a review of its procedures, independence and documentation techniques by another CPA firm every three years. An unsatisfactory finding may result in license suspension.

Because of the additional accounting knowledge and experience, you may want to consult with a CPA when setting up your new business.

SELECTING THE LEGAL ENTITY FOR YOUR BUSINESS: CHECKLIST OF ITEMS TO CONSIDER WHEN FORMING A BUSINESS

Don't feel bad if you feel overwhelmed with all the information and decisions. Some accounting books will try to tell you that **choosing** a legal entity and **setting up an** accounting system is easy. It's a good idea to do some research and more reading. You may even consider an hour or two of consulting time from an attorney or Certified Public Accountant before you get in too deep.

If this sounds silly, here is a list of partial issues to consider when forming a business. It's enough to give an accountant a headache:

	Yes	No
Is limited liability important for me and the other owners?	☐	☐
Should my business have flexible ownership and capital structure?	☐	☐
Should my business have continuity of life?	☐	☐
Should my business have a centralized management?	☐	☐
Should my business have free transferability of ownership interests?	☐	☐
Will my business income be double taxed?	☐	☐
What is the tax treatment of fringe benefits for me and/or other owners?	☐	☐
Do I want my business to have flexibility to select a tax year end?	☐	☐
How do the passive loss rules apply?	☐	☐
Is there a deduction for corporate dividends received?	☐	☐
As an owner, can I take loans against a qualified retirement plan?	☐	☐
Is there a favorable long-term capital gains tax rate?	☐	☐

	Yes	No
Is there double taxation upon the liquidation of my business?	☐	☐
Do the "Personal Holding Company" (PHC) tax rules apply?	☐	☐
Does the accumulated earnings tax apply?	☐	☐
Are there issues regarding "unreasonable owner compensation"?	☐	☐
Do the "Personal Service Corporation" (PSC) tax rules apply?	☐	☐
Are there limitations for the use of the "cash method" of accounting?	☐	☐
Are there limitations for the use of operating losses?	☐	☐
Will my business be subject to Alternative Minimum Tax?	☐	☐
Is there a favorable treatment of my owner interest to acquire stock?	☐	☐
Is there a basis adjustment upon purchase of an ownership interest?	☐	☐
Is there an ability to make tax-free contributions and/or distributions?	☐	☐
Is there an ability to make special tax allocations among owners?	☐	☐
Is there an ability to shift income to my family members?	☐	☐
Is there a possibility of built-in capital gains tax?	☐	☐
Am I taxed on any gain on sales of my ownership interest?	☐	☐
Can I deduct a loss on the sale of my ownership interest?	☐	☐
How have I coordinated my choice of business entity with my estate planning?	☐	☐
Do Section 465 at-risk rules apply?	☐	☐
Do I really want to do this?	☐	☐

Comparison of Different Legal Entities

	Sole Proprietorship	General Partnership	C-Corporation	S-Corporation	LLC
Separate taxable entity	No	No	Yes	No	No
Taxation of income	Directly to owner at their rate	Directly to partners at their rates	Taxed to corporation at sect. 11 rates. Shareholders taxed upon distribution of dividends	Directly to shareholders at their rates. If there is built-in gain the S Corporation is taxed	Directly to members at their rates
Contribution of property in exchange for ownership interests	No gain or loss recognized	No gain or loss recognized unless the contributed property is subject to debt	No gain or loss recognized if transferors are in control of the company after the exchange. Possible exception if contributed property is subject to debt	No gain or loss recognized if transferors are in control of the company after the exchange. Possible exception if contributed property is subject to debt	No gain or loss recognized unless the contributed property is subject to debt

Contribution of services in exchange for ownership interest	N/A	Taxable. Possible exception if ownership interest is only a profits interest	Taxable	Taxable	Taxable
Special allocation of income/loss to partner or shareholder	N/A	Yes, it has substantial economic effect	No	No	Yes, it has substantial economic effect
Distribution to owner	No gain or loss recognized	No gain or loss recognized on distribution of property other than money until partner disposes of the property	Any gain in distributed property taxable to the entity	Distribution of appreciated property results in gain at shareholder level but shareholder gets basis increase	No gain or loss recognized on distribution of property other than money until partner disposes of the property
Character of income and loss	N/A	Character is passed through from entity	Not applicable	Character is passed through from entity	Character is passed through from entity

	Sole Proprietorship	General Partnership	C-Corporation	S-Corporation	LLC
Deduction of losses on owner's tax returns	Yes	Yes. Deductible by partners to extent of basis in partnership interest. A partner's share of debt is reflected in basis. Deductibility may be limited by passive loss and at-risk rules	No. Deductible against corporate income. NOLs generally can be carried back 3 years and carried forward 15 years	Yes. Deductible by shareholders to the extent of basis in stock and loans from shareholder to corporation. Deductibility may be limited by passive loss and at-risk rules	Yes. Deductible by members to extent of basis in member interest. A member's share of debt is reflected in basis. Deductibility may be limited by passive loss and at-risk rules
Maximum number of owners	One (Note: Husband and Wife are treated as one)	Limited by publicly traded partnership rules	No limit	Number of share-holders may not exceed 35	Limited by publicly traded partnership rules
Trust may be an owner	No	Yes	Yes	Limited types of trusts may be shareholders	Yes

Corporation may be an owner	No	Yes	Yes	No. Only individuals, estates and certain trusts may be shareholders	Yes
Limited liability company may be an owner	No	Yes	Yes	No. Only individuals, estates and certain trusts may be shareholders	Yes
Partnership may be an owner	No	Yes	Yes	No. Only individuals, estates and certain trusts may be shareholders	Yes
Nonresident may be an owner	Yes	Yes	Yes	No	Yes
Basic ownership unit	N/A	Partnership interest	Share	Share	Membership interest
Limited Liability	No	No	Yes	Yes	Yes

Comparison of Different Legal Entities (Cont.)

	Sole Proprietorship	General Partnership	C-Corporation	S-Corporation	LLC
Member participation in management	N/A	All partners have equal rights to manage and participate in business except as restricted by partnership agreement	Management of corporation vested in the board of directors. Shareholders elect directors and vote on organic changes	Management of corporation vested in the board of directors. Shareholders elect directors and vote on organic changes	If member managed, yes. If manager managed, no.
Transferability of interest	Must sell entire business or become different entity	Partner may transfer an economic interest in the partnership without consent. Transfer of voting interest requires unanimous consent.	Freely transferable, absent restrictions in stockholder agreement	Freely transferable, absent restrictions in stockholder agreement. However, a transfer to an ineligible pay may result in termination of S Corp. status	Must look at operative agreement
Allocation of profit and loss	All to owner	Per capita	Pro rata to number of shares unless varied by other class of stock	Pro rata to number of shares	Per agreement

Liquidation	No gain or loss	Generally no gain or loss recognized. Gain or loss may be recognized for certain non-pro rata distributions	Corporation and shareholders generally recognize gain or loss	Corporation recognizes gain or loss which is taxed to shareholders	Generally no gain or loss recognized. Gain or loss may be recognized for certain non-pro rata distributions
Fringe benefits	Owner generally not eligible for tax-free fringes	Partners generally not eligible for tax-free fringes	Shareholder employees may receive tax qualified fringe benefits without restriction	Owner of more than 2% of S Corporation shares generally cannot receive tax-free benefits. Expenses for benefits are deductible in computing taxable income but amounts used to purchase benefits for more than 2% shareholders flow through as income to them	Members generally not eligible for tax-free fringes

Comparison of Different Legal Entities (Cont.)

	Sole Proprietorship	General Partnership	C-Corporation	S-Corporation	LLC
Employment taxes	Self-employment tax applies to income	Self-employment tax applies to compensation of partners	FICA tax payable by the corporation and employees	FICA tax payable by the corporation and employees	Self-employment tax applies to income of members
IRS election required	None	None	None	Yes	None
Federal tax return	1040 Schedule	Form 1065	Form 1120	Form 1120-S	Form 1065

2

Registering with the Tax Authorities

A significant task for you as a new business owner is to assure that your business is properly complying with the extensive tax and payroll filing requirements imposed by various governmental agencies. Stiff penalties are commonly assessed if the required forms and returns are not properly prepared and filed on time. There are several forms which need to be filed when (or before) your business is started. While this chapter is not intended to be an all inclusive list of the filing requirements, it summarizes some of the more prominent requirements common to most businesses. Many industries and professions have additional specific filing requirements and licenses which are not part of this text but must not be overlooked. Professionals with experience in your industry should be consulted to assure that any such filings are properly handled.

FEDERAL EMPLOYER
IDENTIFICATION NUMBER (EIN)

Any new partnership, corporation, or Limited Liability Company should obtain a **federal tax identification** number. This is required because your business becomes its own legal entity. If you are starting a new sole proprietorship, you should obtain a federal tax identification number *only* if you intend to hire employees.

All tax forms filed with the Internal Revenue Service will require the use of this Federal Employer Identification Number (EIN). This number can be obtained by filing a *Form SS-4* with the Internal Revenue Service. A sample Form SS-4 follows this section.

There is no deadline for filing Form SS-4. However, to avoid substantial confusion, file your Form SS-4 early. If an income tax return or payment is filed without an EIN, the Internal Revenue Service will assign one. It is not uncommon for the Internal Revenue Service to assign more than one EIN to a business which generates letters from the IRS asking for delinquent tax returns on an EIN which you shouldn't have been issued. If you do not file for an EIN early on, you may end up with a confusing mess. Also, keep in mind that if you become the new owner of an existing business, DO NOT use the EIN of the former owner. You should apply for a new EIN unless you buy the stock of a corporation.

You can apply for an EIN either by mail or by fax. You can get an EIN within a few days by faxing your EIN application to the IRS. If you call the Tele-TIN number for the IRS service center for your state, you will be given the fax number. These IRS numbers are listed at the end of this section. In order to obtain an EIN by fax you must do the following:

Complete a Form SS-4 prior to faxing.

Call only for the issuance of an EIN.

Don't wait until a payment or return is due before obtaining an EIN.

The IRS will fax your EIN number back to you within five days.

The Form SS-4 must be signed by the individual (if a sole proprietorship), a partner, or a corporate officer, or fiduciary of a trust.

STATE TAXING AGENCIES

Your state will have a similar employee identification form which should be filed with an agency like the State Employment Development Department (EDD). This identification number is used at the state level primarily for the reporting of wages and payroll taxes.

You can call information for the nearest State Employment Development Office. They can instruct you on what type of forms you need to submit. There may be several different types of applications depending upon what type of employer you are (i.e., retail sales vs. construction), so they may ask you a few questions.

If you are starting a corporation, the Secretary of State will assign you a Corporate Identification Number upon registration. If you hire employees, you will still need a state EIN for the reporting of wages and payroll taxes. **Don't confuse your corporate ID number with your "employer" ID number.** They are two separate identification numbers.

In addition to your state "employer identification number," you may also need an additional sales tax identification number if your business is involved in any type of taxable sales. You will need to register with the State Board of Equalization. Once this is done, you will be required to file sales tax returns on a regular basis (monthly, quarterly, or annually).

You can call your State Board of Equalization office to obtain an application. Most offices will send it to you in the mail. The application will ask for all types of information about you and your business. It may even ask for personal references as well as a list of three major suppliers. Some states will ask for a monetary deposit. The Sales Tax Board will also make sure you have properly registered with the State Employment Development Department if you intend to hire employees.

COUNTY AGENCIES

The County Tax Assessor may also get involved in your business by assessing a business "property tax" based on the estimated fair market value of the assets used in your business. You will need to call your County Tax Assessor's office and ask whether or not this applies to you. Ask for the Business Section. Many small businesses forget this step. Based on the experiences of the authors, the County Tax Assessor WILL NOT CALL YOU.

Keep in mind that if you do not file the proper information with the County, the Tax Assessor may look to your income tax returns for a listing of assets which can be assessed. In many cases, **small businesses forget to call and are overlooked for years. By the time the Assessor sends you a bill, you are delinquent and assessed with a "penalty" as well as "interest"** *from the date you didn't call them* (i.e., the first day of business). Appealing these additional penalties and taxes is often very frustrating and time consuming, not to mention that you must pay in full, prior to making an appeal.

Remember to notify these offices if you close your business during the course of the year. Otherwise, you will be assessed for a full year of tax versus a partial year.

If you are going to run your business under any other name other than your legal name, you may have to register with the **County office** in which your business will be operating. This is usually the **Fictitious Business Name Office** and will require a personal visit so you can research the name you intend to use. You should have several alternate names in mind in case your first choice has already been issued and registered to someone else. Once you have received clearance, you will have to pay a registration fee. You may also be required to run separate notices in a local newspaper declaring your intent to use this fictitious name. Your county official can direct you to the newspaper applicable to your county. There is a separate charge for this service and the rates vary per newspaper. The requirements for the use of a fictitious business name will vary county to county.

LOCAL

Every level of government becomes involved in the operation of your new business. To operate locally, you must obtain a city business license. Applications can typically be obtained at the city business license office where your business is located. At the time of filing the application, a fee must be paid which can range from $25 to $25,000 depending on the city and size of the business. The license is issued immediately and must be posted in plain sight at your place of business. The license, with the related fee, must be renewed annually.

Some cities require a special license if you have a home office. For example, one city in California requires an additional one-time fee of $125 for each specific address including your home. There is a rather hefty fine for non-compliance. Make sure to ask your city business office about this issue.

IRS TELE-TIN PHONE NUMBERS

These numbers will involve a long distance charge, and should be used ONLY to apply for an Employer Identification Number (EIN). The numbers may change without notice. The IRS representatives at these numbers will instruct you how to apply for your EIN via fax. You can also mail your application to the IRS. Any correspondence should be addressed as in the following sample:

Internal Revenue Service
Attn.: Entity Control
City, State, Zip

If your principal business, office or agency, or legal residence in the case of an individual, is located in:	Call the Tele-TIN phone shown or file with the IRS center as listed below:
Florida, Georgia, South Carolina	Internal Revenue Service Attn: Entity Control Atlanta, GA 39901 (404) 455-2360
New Jersey, New York City and counties of Nassau, Rockland, Suffolk, and Westchester	Holtsville, NY 00501 (516) 447-4955

New York (all other counties), Connecticut, Maine, Massachusetts, New Hampshire, Rhode Island, Vermont	Andover, MA 05001 (508) 474-9717
Illinois, Iowa, Minnesota, Missouri, Wisconsin	Attn.: Entity Control, STOP 57A 2306 E. Bannister Road Kansas City, MO 64131 (816) 926-5999
Delaware, District of Columbia, Maryland, Pennsylvania, Virginia	Philadelphia, PA 19255 (215) 574-2400
Indiana, Kentucky, Michigan, Ohio, West Virginia	Cincinnati, OH 45999 (606) 292-5467
Kansas, New Mexico, Oklahoma, Texas	Austin, TX 73301 (512) 462-7843
Alabama, Arkansas, Louisiana, Mississippi, North Carolina, Tennessee	Memphis, TN 37501 (901) 365-5970
California (all counties not listed below) and Hawaii	Fresno, CA 93888 (209) 452-4010
Alaska, Arizona, California (counties of Alpine, Amador, Butte, Calaveras, Colusa, Contra Costa, Del Norte, El Dorado, Glenn, Humboldt, Lake, Lassen, Marin, Mendocino, Modoc, Napa, Nevada, Placer, Plumas, Sacramento, San Joaquin, Shasta, Sierra, Siskiyou, Solano, Sonoma, Sutter, Tehama, Trinity, Yolo, and Yuba), Colorado, Idaho, Montana, Nebraska, Nevada, North Dakota, Oregon, South Dakota, Utah, Washington, Wyoming	Internal Revenue Service Attn.: Entity Control Mail Stop 5271-T PO Box 9950 Ogden, UT 88409 (801) 620-7645

If you have no legal residence, principal place of business, or principal office or agency in any state, file your form with the Internal Revenue Service Center, Philadelphia, PA 19255 or call (215) 574-2400.

Form **SS-4** (Rev. December 1995) Department of the Treasury Internal Revenue Service	**Application for Employer Identification Number** (For use by employers, corporations, partnerships, trusts, estates, churches, government agencies, certain individuals, and others. See instructions.) ▶ Keep a copy for your records.	EIN _____ OMB No. 1545-0003

<table>
<tr><td rowspan="5">Please type or print clearly.</td><td colspan="2">1 Name of applicant (Legal name) (See instructions.)</td></tr>
<tr><td>2 Trade name of business (if different from name on line 1)</td><td>3 Executor, trustee, "care of" name</td></tr>
<tr><td>4a Mailing address (street address) (room, apt., or suite no.)</td><td>5a Business address (if different from address on lines 4a and 4b)</td></tr>
<tr><td>4b City, state, and ZIP code</td><td>5b City, state, and ZIP code</td></tr>
<tr><td colspan="2">6 County and state where principal business is located</td></tr>
</table>

7 Name of principal officer, general partner, grantor, owner, or trustor - SSN required (See instructions.) ▶ _____

8a Type of entity (Check only one box.) (See instructions.)

☐ Sole Proprietor (SSN) _____
☐ Partnership   ☐ Personal service corp.
☐ REMIC   ☐ Limited liability co.
☐ State/local government   ☐ National Guard
☐ Other nonprofit organization (specify) ▶
☐ Other (specify) ▶

☐ Estate (SSN of decedent) _____
☐ Plan administrator - SSN _____
☐ Other corporation (specify) ▶
☐ Trust   ☐ Farmers' cooperative
☐ Federal Government/military ☐ Church or church-controlled organization
(enter GEN if applicable) _____

8b If a corporation, name the state or foreign country (if applicable) where incorporated | State | Foreign country

9 Reason for applying (Check only one box.)

☐ Started new business (specify) ▶
☐ Hired employees
☐ Created a pension plan (specify type) ▶

☐ Banking purpose (specify) ▶
☐ Changed type of organization (specify) ▶
☐ Purchased going business
☐ Created a trust (specify) ▶
☐ Other (specify) ▶

10 Date business started or acquired (Mo., day, year) (See instructions.) | **11** Closing month of accounting year (See instructions.)

12 First date wages or annuities were paid or will be paid (Mo., day, year). **Note:** *If applicant is a withholding agent, enter date income will first be paid to nonresident alien. (Mo., day, year)* . . . . ▶

13 Highest number of employees expected in the next 12 months. **Note:** *If the applicant does not expect to have any employees during the period, enter -0-. (See instructions.)* . . . . ▶ | Nonagricultural | Agricultural | Household

14 Principal activity (See instructions.) ▶

15 Is the principal business activity manufacturing? . . . . ☐ Yes ☐ No
If "Yes," principal product and raw material used ▶

16 To whom are most of the products or services sold? Please check the appropriate box. ☐ Business (wholesale)
☐ Public (retail)   ☐ Other (specify) ▶   ☐ N/A

17a Has the applicant ever applied for an identification number for this or any other business? . . . . ☐ Yes ☐ No
Note: *If "Yes," please complete lines 17b and 17c.*

17b If you checked "Yes" on line 17a, give applicant's legal name and trade name shown on prior application, if different from line 1 or 2 above.

Legal name ▶   Trade name ▶

17c Approximate date when and city and state where the application was filed. Enter previous employer identification number if known.

Approximate date when filed (Mo., day, year)	City and State where filed	Previous EIN

Under penalties of perjury, I declare that I have examined this application, and to the best of my knowledge and belief, it is true, correct, and complete. | Business telephone number (include area code)
 | Fax telephone number (include area cod

Name and title (Please type or print clearly.) ▶

Signature ▶   Date ▶

Note: *Do not write below this line. For official use only.*

Please leave blank ▶	Geo.	Ind.	Class	Size	Reason for applying

For Paperwork Reduction Act Notice, see page 4.   Form **SS-4** (Rev. 12-9

JSA

General Instructions

Section references are to the Internal Revenue Code unless otherwise noted.

Purpose of Form

Use Form SS4 to apply for an employer identification number (EIN). An EIN is a nine-digit number (for example, 12-3456789) assigned to sole proprietors, corporations, partnerships, estates, trusts, and other entities for filing and reporting purposes. The information you provide on this form will establish your filing and reporting requirements.

Who Must File

You must file this form if you have not obtained an EIN before and:

- You pay wages to one or more employees including household employees.

- You are required to have an EIN to use on any return, statement, or other document, even if you are not an employer.

- You are a withholding agent required to withhold taxes on income, other than wages, paid to a nonresident alien (individual, corporation, partnership, etc.). A withholding agent may be an agent, broker, fiduciary, manager, tenant, or spouse, and is required to file **Form 1042,** Annual Withholding Tax Return for U.S. Source Income of Foreign Persons.

- You file **Schedule C,** Profit or Loss From **Business,** or **Schedule F,** Profit or Loss From Farming, of **Form 1040,** U.S. Individual Income Tax Return, **and** have a Keogh plan or are required to file excise, employment, information, or alcohol, tobacco, or firearms returns.

The following must use EINs even if they do not have any employees:

- State and local agencies who serve as tax reporting agents for public assistance recipients, under Rev. Proc. 809, 1980-1 C.B. 581, should obtain a separate EIN for this reporting. See **Household employer**.

- Trusts, except the following:

    1. Certain grantor-owned revocable trusts. (See the **Instructions for Form 1041.**)

    2. Individual Retirement Arrangement (IRA) trusts, unless the trust has to file **Form 990-T,** Exempt Organization Business Income Tax Return. (See the **Instructions for Form 990-T.**)

    3. Certain trusts that are considered household employers can use the trust EIN to report and pay the social security and Medicare taxes, Federal unemployment tax (FUTA) and withheld Federal income tax. A separate EIN is not necessary.

- Estates

- Partnerships

- REMICs (real estate mortgage investment conduits) (See the **Instructions for Form 1066,** U.S. Real Estate Mortgage Investment Conduit Income Tax Return.)

- Corporations

- Nonprofit organizations (churches, clubs, etc.)

-Farmers' cooperatives

- Plan administrators (A plan administrator is the person or group of persons specified as the administrator by the instrument under which the plan is operated.)

When To Apply for a New EIN

New Business. - If you become the new owner of an existing business, do not use the EIN of the former owner. IF YOU ALREADY HAVE AN EIN, USE THAT NUMBER. If you do not have an EIN, apply for one on this form. If you become the "owner" of a corporation by acquiring its stock, use the corporation's EIN.

Changes in Organization or Ownership. - If you already have an EIN, you may need to get a new one if either the organization or ownership of your business changes. If you incorporate a sole proprietorship or form a partnership, you must get a new EIN. However, do not apply for a new EIN if you change only the name of your business.

Note: *If you are electing to be an "S corporation," be sure you file* **Form 2553,** *Election by a Small Business Corporation.*

File Only One Form SS-4. - File only one Form SS-4, regardless of the number of businesses operated or trade names under which a business operates. However, each corporation in an affiliated group must file a separate application.

EIN Applied For, But Not Received. - If you do not have an EIN by the time a return is due, write "Applied for" and the date you applied in the space shown for the number. **Do not** show your social security number as an EIN on returns.

If you do not have an EIN by the time a tax deposit is due, send your payment to the Internal Revenue Service Center for your filing area. (See **Where To Apply** below.) Make your check or money order payable to Internal Revenue Service and show your name (as shown on Form SS-4), address, type of tax, period covered, and date you applied for an EIN. Send an explanation with the deposit.

For more information about EINs, see **Pub. 583,** Starting a Business and Keeping Records, and **Pub. 1635,** Understanding Your EIN.

How To Apply

You can apply for an EIN either by mail or by telephone. You can get an EIN immediately by calling the Tele-TIN phone number for the service center for your state, or you can send the completed Form SS-4 directly to the service center to receive your EIN in the mail.

Application by Tele-TIN. - Under the Tele-TIN program, you can receive your EIN over the telephone and use it immediately to file a return or make a payment. To receive an EIN by phone, complete Form SS-4, then call the Tele-TIN phone number listed for your state under **Where To Apply.** The person making the call must be authorized to sign the form. (See **Signature block.**)

An IRS representative will use the information from the Form SS-4 to establish your account and assign you an EIN. Write the number you are given on the upper right-hand corner of the form, sign and date it.

*Mail or FAX the signed SS-4 **within 24 hours** to the Tele-TIN Unit at the service center address for your state.* The IRS representative will give you the FAX number. The FAX numbers are also listed in Pub. 1635.

Taxpayer representatives can receive their client's EIN by phone if they first send a facsimile (FAX) of a completed **Form 2848,** Power of Attorney and Declaration of Representative, or **Form 8821,** Tax Information Authorization, to the Tele-TIN unit. The **Form 2848** or **Form 8821** will be used solely to release the EIN to the representative authorized on the form.

Application by Mail. - Complete Form SS-4 at least 4 to 5 weeks before you will need an EIN. Sign and date the application and mail it to the service center address for your state. You will receive your EIN in the mail in approximately 4 weeks.

Where To Apply

The Tele-TIN phone numbers listed below will involve a long-distance charge to callers outside of the local calling area and can be used only to apply for an EIN. THE NUMBERS MAY CHANGE WITHOUT NOTICE. Use 1-800-829-1040 to verify a number or to ask about an application by mail or other Federal tax matters.

If your principal business office or agency, or legal residence in the case of an individual, is located in:	Call the Tele-TIN phone number shown or file with the Internal Revenue Service Center at:
Florida, Georgia, South Carolina	Attn: Entity Control Atlanta, GA 39901 (404) 455-2360
New Jersey, New York City and counties of Nassau, Rockland, Suffolk and Westchester	Attn: Entity Control Holtsville, NY 00501 (516) 447-4955
New York (all other counties), Connecticut, Maine, Massachusetts New Hampshire, Rhode Island, Vermont	Attn: Entity Control Andover, MA 05501 (508) 474-9717
Illinois, Iowa, Minnesota, Missouri, Wisconsin	Attn: Entity Control Stop 57A 2306 E. Bannister Rd. Kansas City, MO 64131 (816) 926-5999
Delaware, District of Columbia, Maryland, Pennsylvania, Virginia	Attn: Entity Control Philadelphia, PA 19255 (215) 574-2400
Indiana, Kentucky, Michigan, Ohio, West Virginia	Attn: Entity Control Cincinnati, OH 45999 (606) 292-5467
Kansas, New Mexico, Oklahoma, Texas	Attn: Entity Control Austin, TX 73301 (512) 460-7843
Alaska, Arizona, California, (counties of Alpine, Amador, Butte, Calaveras, Colusa, Contra Costa, Del Norte, El Dorado, Glenn, Humboldt, Lake, Lassen, Marin, Mendocino, Modoc, Napa, Nevada, Placer, Plumas, Sacramento, San Joaquin, Shasta, Sierra, Siskiyou, Solona, Sonoma, Sutter, Tehama, Trinity, Yolo, and Yuba), Colorado, Idaho, Montana, Nebraska, Nevada, North Dakota, Oregon, South Dakota, Utah, Washington, Wyoming	Attn: Entity Control Mail Stop 6271-T P.O. Box 9950 Ogden, UT 84409 (801) 620-7645
California (all other counties), Hawaii	Attn: Entity Control Fresno, CA 93888 (209) 452-4010
Alabama, Arkansas, Louisiana, Mississippi, North Carolina, Tennessee	Attn: Entity Control Memphis, TN 37501 (901) 365-5970

If you have no legal residence, principal place of business, or principal office or agency in any state, file your form with the Internal Revenue Service Center, Philadelphia, PA 19255 or call 215-574-2400.

CHECKLIST: REGISTERING WITH THE TAX AUTHORITIES

Task	Date Begun	Person Contacted	Outcome
1. If you are forming a partnership or corporation, obtain a federal EIN immediately.			
2. If you are a sole proprietorship and plan to hire employees, obtain a federal EIN immediately.			
3. If you are hiring employees, call the State Employment Development Department. You will need a state "employer identification number."			
4. Make sure to contact any other State office which might regulate your industry or professional license.			
5. Make sure to obtain a sales tax identification number if your business involves sales of any type.			
6. Call your County Tax Assessor's office and verify whether or not there are any taxes assessed on business property.			
7. Determine whether there are any county or state restrictions on the use of a fictitious name.			
8. Register with your City Business license office. Inquire about various locations and home in office, if applicable.			

3

Keeping the Books

One of your biggest difficulties in starting your new business is maintaining the accounting and bookkeeping functions. This is due to the fact that you are probably an outstanding sales person, mechanic, dentist, or inventor with little or no training in the field of accounting. The situation becomes extremely hazardous when you purchase a computer and accounting program and try to "go it alone."

As a business owner you might feel that you can rely on your "gut feeling" about where you are making or losing money. In most situations, however, you have embarked on a new business primarily out of love for a profession or the enthusiasm of *"I can build a better mouse trap."* These "emotional overlays" can often cloud your decision making.

Accurate and TIMELY record keeping will allow you to make proper decisions based on the actual information of your company. Your company's books and financial statements represent a score sheet which will tell you how you are progressing and will provide you with early warning signals to let you know when and why your business may be going under.

The necessity for well organized and TIMELY financial records cannot be over-emphasized.

ACCOUNTS

As with any profession, accounting has its own theories, guidelines, and terminology. It is important to understand that accounting, just like chemistry and physics, has its own unique theory which needs to be accepted before you can proceed to the next level of application. As in chemistry, you need to accept the fact water is represented by H_2O (two hydrogen molecules and one oxygen molecule). There is no particular rhyme or reason, except that's just the way it is. Accounting and its theory is very similar. Cash is always a resource, and is normally represented by a debit balance. There is no particular rhyme or reason. That's just the way it is.

Once you have memorized or accepted this accounting theory without trying to figure out "why," you are on your way to applying it to your business. Once you are able to understand some of the terminology, the process of recording transactions becomes easier.

One of the more fundamental accounting terms is called an "account." This is a term used to describe an individual accounting item. An "account" represents the various increases and decreases to a specific assets, liability or equity item of your business. Your business can use as many accounts as necessary in order to provide the detailed information you need. The accounting items or "accounts" are divided into eight major categories as follows:

Accounting Category	Types of Accounts
assets	These are things or resources your business owns. The types of accounts may be "cash," "inventory," "furniture," "vehicles," etc.
liabilities	These are debts payable to others such as a bank loan payable, amounts payable to your vendors/creditors, amounts payable for sales taxes,

	or even amounts owed to your employees. Your accounts might be "bank loan payable" or "taxes payable."
equity	This is the difference between your assets and your liabilities. Type of equity accounts might be "common stock" or "proprietor's capital," "retained earnings" or "owner's equity."
income	This is the money received from the sale of merchandise, the performance of a service, or the rental of property. Income accounts might be "merchandise sales" or "installation fees." Remember that cash received from a loan is the result of a note which becomes payable. This is probably the most common error small businesses make. Transferring funds does not result in income either. It is merely moving funds from one cash account to another cash account.
cost of sales	These are the direct costs related to the sale of merchandise or the performance of the service. These accounts might be "raw materials," "commissions," or "delivery expenses."
expense	These are the general operating expenses incurred to run your business. Expense "accounts" might include "rents," "telephone," "utilities," and "office supplies," and "interest expense." Remember, that repayment of loans are not an expense. This is because the amount received was not income. (See the income paragraph above.) This is another common error small businesses make. The interest on the loan is an expense, but not the repayment of the loan principal.
other income	This is revenue that is not part of your everyday income such as interest income or special one time sale of assets. An example of this type of account might be "interest income."
other expense	These are costs or expenses that are not related to the sale of merchandise or the running of your business. This is reserved for the unusual and infrequent type of expense. An example of this account might be "flood loss."

Each major accounting category has a list of "accounts" which are designed to record any increase or decrease in each of the items. This is possible because each account has a debit and credit side. When you want to know the status of your "cash account," you can merely take your beginning cash amount, add up all the increases, subtract the decreases, and determine the ending balance. As you will find out later, the ending balances of each of these accounts is assembled periodically (monthly is good) in order to prepare the financial statements for your business.

In order to make things easier, the accounts are usually summarized in some systematic manner that represents the way they would show up on the financial statements. The accounts are usually assigned a numeric number and are kept in financial statement sequence. An example of a chart of accounts is shown at page 42.

DEBITS AND CREDITS

Now that you have accounts which can be used for recording increases or decreases, you must learn the concept of debits and credits. Remember, debits and credits are not the same as "plus" or "minus." They are simply words that mean "left" or "right."

Accounting is based on a theory that business transactions result in a financially equal equation. In the ancient world of Babylonian traders, a line was often drawn in the sand. A trader would move his chicken and cow to one side of the line, as long as baskets and grain were received in exchange. This business transaction was equal as long as both parts of the transaction occurred (i.e., the chicken and cow moved to the left of the line; and the baskets and grain moved to the right). The records of ancient Babylon, inscribed on soft clay tablets, date back to over four thousand years ago. These are the earliest known commercial accounting records.

the left side of the line	*the right side of the line*
cow and chicken	baskets and grain

Although trading and sales have become more sophisticated, the basic theory of an equal transaction still holds true. In today's world, you, the business owner, are willing to exchange your cash (an asset) for a crate of #2 egg cartons (a packaging expense). The value of the exchange must be equal or neither party will finalize the deal. The accounting process tries to record this "deal" or transaction. If you had your "line in the sand," the transaction would look something like this:

the left side of the line	*the right side of the line*
#2 egg cartons (which you received)	cash (which you gave up)

You can now use your individual "accounts" to record this transaction to the accounting record. Transactions on the LEFT are called "DEBITS" and transactions on the RIGHT are called "CREDITS." These terms mean nothing more than left or right. Each asset, liability, equity, income and expense account has a debt side and a credit side. One of the fundamental things to remember as you are doing your accounting is that DEBITS MUST EQUAL CREDITS FOR EACH TRANSACTION.

From the accounting prospective, your business transaction to purchase the #2 egg cartons will be recorded in a journal as follows:

	Debit	Credit
12/5/99–Record purchase of egg cartons		
Packaging Expense (account name for an expense)	$20.00	
Cash (account name for an asset)		$20.00

Because debits and credits don't follow any obvious rule, it is difficult to remember which accounts normally have a debit balance and which normally have a credit balance.

The following chart shows the accounts and the sign they "*normally*" carry.

Account	Normal Sign	Description
Assets	Debit	All the recourses a business owns
Liabilities	Credit	All debts/payables a business owes
Equity	Credit	The difference between what is owned and what is owed
Income	Credit	The money received for products and/or services sold
Cost of Sales	Debit	The direct costs of products and/or services sold
Expenses	Debit	The money paid for costs necessary to operate your business

Since each account has a debit and credit side, they are affected by both the debits and credits. The effects of debits and credits are summarized as follows:

A debit indicates:	A credit indicates:
assets increase	assets decrease
liability decrease	**liability increase**
equity or proprietorship decrease	equity or proprietorship increase
income decrease	**income increase**
expense increase	expense decrease

THE JOURNAL

Your recording process will begin with a transaction. This is the economic event (such as a sale of merchandise or the purchase of the #2 egg cartons) that needs to be recorded. Transactions need to be recorded in a chronological order. This can be done manually on a sheet of paper, in a notebook, or by a computer and becomes known as the "journal." This is also known as the book of original entry.

A/R = Current Assets

A smaller start up company might simply have a *cash receipts journal* to record all the cash receipt/sales transactions, and a *cash disbursements journal* which shows all the disbursement transactions. These journals will provide the chronological record of your sales or cash disbursements AND disclose the complete transaction (which needs a "DEBIT" and "CREDIT" part). There are several types of journals such as the *cash receipts journal, the cash disbursements journal, the sales journal, the purchases journal, the accounts receivable journal, the accounts payable journal,* and *the general journal.* The nature and size of your business will determine the number and types of journals you have.

Entering your transactions to the journal is known as "journalizing." Before a transaction can be recorded in a journal, it is necessary to analyze the transaction and decide what accounts should be debited and what accounts should be credited. In this regard, "journalizing" really refers to (1) an analysis of the transaction and (2) actually recording it in the journal.

An entry into a journal normally contains the following seven parts:

1. *The date*—make sure to include the year.
2. *Titles of accounts to be debited*—care should be exercised to use the exact account titles. This will avoid confusion where names of the accounts are somewhat similar.
3. *Debit amount*—the dollar amount is entered in the left hand column opposite the respective account titles.
4. *Title of accounts to be credited*—the title to the account being credited is always underneath the debit item—but always indented from the left edge so that it won't be confused with a debit description.
5. *Credit amount*—the dollar amount is entered in the right hand column opposite the account title.
6. *Explanation*—it is always recommended that you write in a brief explanation. It should be brief, but sufficient enough to help you recall the particulars of the transaction should you need to investigate at a later date.

7. *Reference*—you may want to include a reference column that references your transaction to a particular invoice number, etc. In a disbursement journal where you record cash being disbursed, you can use the check number as a reference. These entries are helpful later on if you are trying to analyze and track down an incorrect entry.

Sample entries into a *sales journal:*

Corena's Chicken Company Sales Journal For 1999

Date	Account Title/Explanation	Ref/ Inv#	Debit	Credit
ENTRY #1—Sold ten dozen eggs to Gail's Gourmet Gingersnaps				
12/1/99	Cash	001	$100.00	
	Sales			$100.00
ENTRY #2—Sold forty-five chickens to Gary's very large family.				
12/7/99	Cash	002	$450.00	
	Sales			$450.00

The reference numbers in this example are the respective invoice numbers.

Sample entries into a *disbursement journal:*

Corena's Chicken Company Disbursement Journal For 1999

Date	Account Title/Explanation	Check#	Debit	Credit
ENTRY #1—Buy food for the feathered friends.				
12/1/99	Chicken Feed Expense	555	$ 100.00	
	Cash			$100.00
ENTRY #2—Bought a new tractor (finally!).				
	Made cash down pymnt, bank financed balance.			
12/3/99	Tractor equipment *Asset*	556	$6,000.00	
	Cash			$ 500.00
	Note Payable to bank			5,500.00

The reference numbers in this example are the respective check numbers. Whenever three or more accounts are required to record an entry, it is known as a compound entry. In a compound entry it is important that your total debit and credit amounts are equal. Also, the traditional format requires that all debits are listed first, before the credit entries.

THE LEDGER

After you have entered items into your journals, your second step is to record into a ledger. The ledger is the book of second entry. It is a derived record which shows the analytical activity for each account. You will notice that the disbursement journal shows all disbursements. The sales journal shows all the sales. Having a ledger is similar to having an "activity" card for each and every one of your accounts. In this regard, your ledger card for "tractor equipment" would only show the purchase of the tractor with a line item entry showing the $6,000 debit. The ledger card for "tractor equipment" would not show any other activity. The cash ledger, on the other hand, would show only the cash activity.

Of course, recording this $6,000 debit to the "equipment ledger card," means that you must record a credit somewhere. If you look back to the journal entry, you will see that the credit will be posted to two different ledger cards—the card for cash, and the card for notes payable to the bank.

This transferring of this information from the journal to the appropriate "activity card" is called "posting." It isn't more complex than a copying procedure. If you are doing this manually, you will usually be "posting" from one accounting sheet to another. Keep in mind that you may not have an actual ledger "card." A ledger can also be kept using a looseleaf binder or a large bound book. What is important is that each ledger sheet/card shows only the activity for one account. It is important to remember that this copying process leaves room for lots of errors. Numbers are easily transposed or recorded in the wrong columns. These errors will surface when you prepare a trial balance and find that it doesn't "balance."

If you are working with a computerized system, this problem will not occur. Once you have input the basic data from the journals (i.e., sales, cash receipts, cash disbursements, etc.) the computer will merge and "post" all the information to the appropriate ledger and produce the trial balance and financial statements.

Once your sales journal has been "posted" to your general ledger, you can determine the status of your various accounts at month end by reviewing the general ledger card/sheet for each account. A look at the Chicken Company Ledger Sheet reveals the following:

Corena's Chicken Company General Ledger Sheet—Cash
For the year 1999

Date	Explanation	Ref	Debit	Credit
12/1/99	Cash received	INV#1	$100.00	
12/1/99	Chicken Feed purchased			$100.00
12/3/99	Tractor down payment			$500.00
12/5/99	Egg cartons purchased			$ 20.00
12/7/99	Cash received	INV#2	$450.00	
	Sub-totals		$550.00	$620.00
	Ending overall balance			($70.00)

Keep in mind that cash normally has an ending debit balance. The credit of $70.00 means that Corena has overdrawn her account (again!).

Corena's Chicken Company General Ledger Sheet—Sales
For the year 1999

Date	Explanation	Ref	Debit	Credit
12/1/99	Sold stuff to Gail	INV#1		$100.00
12/3/99	Sold stuff to Gary	INV#2		$450.00
	Sub-totals			$550.00

Keep in mind that the sales account normally has an ending credit balance.

Corena's Chicken Company
General Ledger Sheet—Packaging Expense
For the year 1999

Date	Explanation	Ref	Debit	Credit
12/5/99	Bought egg cartons	CHK#557	$20.00	
	Sub-totals		$20.00	

Keep in mind that expense accounts normally have an ending debit balance.

THE ACCOUNTING FORMULA IN ACTION

Working through a series of transactions will help you to understand which account items are affected and how the entry should be made. When you are making your accounting entries you need to ask yourself what happened, what was the sequence, where did the information come from, where did it go. An accounting transaction is an event that causes a change in assets, liabilities, or the owner's equity. Since our basic accounting formula must always be maintained, a change in one item affects an equal change in another item or items. As with our previous example, a decrease in assets (chicken and cow) resulted in an increase in other assets (baskets and grain).

Keep the accounting formula in mind as you work through the following transactions:

Assets   =   Liabilities   +   Owner's Equity

1. You invest $10,000 cash to start your business. There is an increase in cash and an increase in owner's equity.

Assets	=	Liabilities	+	Owner's Equity
(Cash)				(Original Investment)
$10,000	=	-0-	+	$10,000

2. You buy furniture for $3,000 cash. There is a decrease in cash and an increase in another asset called furniture.

Assets	=	Liabilities	+	Owner's Equity
Cash + Furniture	=	-0-	+	(Original Investment)
$10,000				$10,000
(3,000) + $3,000	=	-0-	+	$10,000
$ 7,000 + $3,000	=	-0-	+	$10,000

3. You buy a computer for $4,000 on credit. There is an increase in assets and an increase in liabilities.

Assets	=	Liabilities + Owner's Equity
Cash + Furn. + Computer		
$7,000 + $3,000	=	-0- + $10,000
+ $4,000	=	$4,000
$7,000 + $3,000 + $4,000	=	$4,000 + $10,000

4. You withdraw $2,000 in cash for your personal use. There is a decrease in cash and a decrease in your owner's equity.

Assets	=	Liabilities + Owner's Equity
Cash + Furn. + Computer=	Liabilities	+ Initial Investment
$7,000 + $3,000 + $4,000 =	$4,000	+ $10,000
(2,000) =		(2,000)
$5,000 + $3,000 + $4,000 =	$4,000	+ $8,000

5. You perform services to a customer for $2,500. You receive $2,500 in cash.

Assets	= Liabilities+	Owner's Equity
Cash + Furn. + Computer =	Loan payable	+ O/E + Rev. − Expn
$5,000 + $3,000 + $4,000 =	$4,000	+ $8,000
+ 2,500		+ $2,500
$7,500 + $3,000 + $4,000 =	$4,000	+ $8,000 + $2,500

6. You sell a dozen eggs to Gail's Gourmet Gingersnap Company on credit (not for cash).

Assets				= Liabilities	+ Owner's Equity		
Cash +	Accts. Receiv.	+ Furn.	+ Comp. =	Loan payable	+ O/E	+ Rev.	− Expn
$7,500 +	-0-	+ $3,000	+ $4,000 =	$4,000	+ $8,000	+ $2,500	
+	2,500					+ $2,500	
$7,500 +	$2,500 +	$3,000	+ $4,000 =	$4,000	+ $8,000	+ $5,000	

As you have probably already concluded, proper planning in the set up of your accounting system is critical. The effectiveness of your new system is dependent on something which is well thought out. Your most effective use of an accountant or bookkeeper would be for the set up phase. You may also want to refer to the following checklist to assist with this initial process as well.

CHECKLIST: INITIAL ACCOUNTING STEPS FOR STARTING YOUR BUSINESS

Task	Date Began	Date Completed
1. Determine whether or not you will be keeping your books manually or on computer.		
2. Call a local CPA and ask for recommendations for software programs. A recommendation by one of the authors is Mind Your Own Business (MYOB). It is available for both MAC and IBM clone systems.		
3. If you are using your current computer or thinking of buying a new one, make sure your hard drive has enough memory to facilitate your accounting program as well as the accounting data.		
4. Before you draft your chart of accounts, ask yourself what financial information you will need to make effective management decisions.		
5. What accounting information do you need to provide to the various government and taxing authorities (such as total sales to the sales tax board).		
6. Draft a "chart of accounts" and list every account that may possibly affect your business. You need to think into the future a few years and make sure your list will facilitate growth or change.		

Date Task	Date Began	Completed
7. Consider having a bookkeeper or CPA review your chart of accounts.		
8. Make a list of your beginning assets that you are bringing into your business and the estimated market value. An example will be:		

Acct title	*$Amt or Value*	
Cash	Use balance you transfer or make available to your business.	
Furniture and equipment	market value	
Inventory	market value	
Debt	loan balance	

This will be the opening entry on your books. You are transferring these assets and liabilities to your business. The difference between the assets and liabilities will be the contribution (an equity account).

9. Read Chapters 4 and 5 and find out whether your accounting issues are more complex than you think. Especially in terms of "inventory" or the use of "cash vs. accrual" accounting method.		
10. Determine if you need to hire someone to assist you with your bookkeeping. Call a CPA for recommendations.		

SAMPLE CHART OF ACCOUNTS

Corena's Chicken Company
100 Main Street
Somewhere, USA
Chart of Accounts

1-000 Assets

1-1000	General Checking
1-1100	Payroll Checking
1-2000	Inventory
1-3000	Accounts Receivable
1-4000	Office Equipment
1-5000	Vehicles
1-6000	Other Assets

2-000 Liabilities

2-1000	Trade Accounts Payable
2-2000	Bank Loan Payable
2-3000	Credit Cards Payable
2-4000	Payroll Taxes Payable
2-5000	Sales Tax Payable

3-000 Equity

3-1000	Owner Beginning Balance
3-2000	Owner Contribution
3-3000	Owner Draws
3-9999	Current Year Earnings

4-000 Income

4-1000	Retail Sales of Eggs
4-2000	Wholesale Sales of Chickens
4-3000	Misc. sales

5-000 Cost of Goods Sold

5-1000	Cost of Chickens
5-2000	Cost of Materials and Supplies
5-3000	Wages for the production labor
5-4000	Commission on sales
5-5000	Other costs

6-000 Operating Expenses

6-1000	Advertising
6-2000	Bank Charges
6-2500	Bookkeeping Fees
6-3000	Depreciation Expn.
6-3500	Equipment rental
6-4000	Freight
6-4500	Insurance
6-5000	Interest Expense
6-5500	Legal and Professional
6-5750	License
6-6000	Office Expense
6-6500	Payroll Taxes
6-7000	Property Taxes
6-7500	Repairs
6-8000	Supplies
6-8500	Telephone
6-9000	Utilities

8-000 Other Income

8-1000	Interest Income

9-000 Other Expenses

9-1000	Flood Loss

4

The Financial Statements

Now that you have some basic idea of the fundamental theory of accounting, you must determine how you can best convert the recording process into financial statements.

Most small business owners make the mistake of thinking they can do everything themselves, including the accounting work. You might be able to build a better mouse trap, but can you still do the marketing, order the supplies, manage the warehouse, review all appropriate insurance coverages, read up on OSHA, build the trap, manage the employees, keep the clients happy and still have time for billing, banking and data entry? **The amount of time required to keep good financial records especially payroll is almost always under-estimated and usually under-valued.** As a result, the record keeping is often a low priority and something "to be caught up with later." This approach can get you into trouble. For example, in some states, if you fail to file a corporate tax return, your corporate status may be suspended (meaning you can no longer do business) and you may be subject to a $1,000 penalty or year in jail, or both. The nasty details involving payroll/accounting problems can be found in Chapter 5.

Keeping up with your daily accounting work and preparing month-end financial statements is a good habit to get into.

THE RECORDING PROCESS

The first step in designing your accounting system is developing a chart of accounts which will establish the framework for your entire data base of accounting information. You have done this already in Chapter 3.

The recording process is a series of steps which will provide you with the final product—a financial statement. Your steps are as follows:

1. Recording entries to a journal—i.e., journalizing (Chapter 3)
2. Recording the journal to a general ledger—i.e., posting (Chapter 3)
3. Summarizing the ending account balances for a trial balance
4. Analyzing the ending balances
5. Making adjust entries if necessary
6. Preparing the final financial statements (balance sheet and profit and loss).

In Chapter 3, you made journal entries to record the transaction of Corena's Chicken Company. You also posted these entries to a general ledger. Your next step will be to prepare the "trial balance."

THE TRIAL BALANCE

A trial balance is a list of all of your accounts and their ending balances at a given time. This should usually be prepared at the end of each month, but it can be done at any time. The primary purpose of the trial balance is to prove the mathematical equality of the debts and credits after posting to the journal. If you have made an error and only posted the debit side of a transaction, your trial balance will not balance. You will be out of balance by the missing credit. A trial balance is a necessary check point before proceeding to the other steps in preparing a financial statement.

Keep in mind that a trial balance does not prove that your ending balances or the transactions you have recorded are accurate. For example, a trial balance may balance even when (1) an entire transaction has been left out, (2) a transaction has been posted twice, or (3) you posted your transaction to the wrong account (i.e., you posted something to telephone and it should have been advertising).

Most computer systems will not allow you to journalize or post unless your debits equal your credits. As a result, your trial balance will always "balance." The greater problem in computerized systems is determining whether or not the information has been posted to the correct account. Because transactions are harder to trace on the computer, you must be sure to print out all underlying journals, ledgers, and detailed trial balances on a monthly basis. All of these reports should be printed at the same time. This way the detail journals will match the balance sheets. Some computer programs often produce month-end journals that do not agree to the financial statements merely because these reports were not printed on the same date. With these programs, once you have missed the end of the month for report printing, you cannot go back. The computer can actually be the most dangerous piece of equipment your business owns. Financial information which has been processed by someone only slightly familiar with computers and accounting often produces inaccurate financial statements which merely have a neat appearance. All you have done is generate bad information more quickly and more neatly. Within the accounting industry this is known as "garbage in—garbage out."

The important thing to keep in mind is that **the numbers on the trial balance mean something.** Many small business owners and bookkeepers often fail to look closely at the trial balance and verify the accuracy of the ending balance. It's amazing how many are surprised that the cash on the trial balance should actually match the cash on the reconciled bank statement. A sample of a bank reconciliation is shown at page 54.

Once you have prepared a trial balance, the individual account items need to be analyzed and compared to additional sources of information to verify their accuracy. For example:

Ending Balance per Trial Balance	**Verified with**
Cash on your trial balance	This should agree to the amount on your reconciled or balanced bank statement.
Accounts Receivable	This should agree to the list of billing for which you haven't received cash payment.
Inventory	This should match your inventory list and the actual amount you have in your warehouse/storage. You should confirm with a physical count of inventory at least annually.
Equipment	This should agree to your equipment list which should be verified with a physical inspection of the equipment.
Bank loan payable	This should match the loan schedule or the payment coupon that shows the amount still owed.
Accounts Payable	This should agree to all the unpaid bills you owe vendors, etc., as of the trial balance date.
Wage Expense	The total wage expense should match the "gross" wages on your Quarterly Payroll tax returns. Most businesses mistakenly show only the net checks as a wage expense. Hence, wages are understated. On the flip side, the payroll tax expense is overstated because it incorrectly includes all the money withheld from the checks. The payroll tax expense is only the employer's share of taxes. See Chapter 6.

ADJUSTING JOURNAL ENTRIES

When analyzing your trial balance, you may note that the ending account balances do not agree to the actual amounts. For example, the cash on your trial balance may not agree with the actual cash on your bank reconciliation. Similarly, the inventory on your trial balance may not agree with your actual inventory list. When this happens, you need to analyze why there is a difference and make an adjustment.

Whenever you have such an error, you must make an adjustment with an adjusting journal entry (AJE). The adjusting entry can then be (1) recorded in your general journal, (2) posted to your ledger, and ultimately (3) summarized on the new revised trial balance. This should be a standard part of your accounting process.

With a computerized system, most of the errors occur because the entry has been posted to the wrong account, or worse, to the wrong year. A review of your detailed trial balance at month end will help you spot erroneous entries. After you have made your adjusting entries, and the ending numbers on your trial balance have been verified to be accurate, you can then prepare your Balance Sheet and Income Statement.

You may want to get in the habit of having your accountant review your financial statements on a quarterly basis to check for errors. Keep in mind that your tax liability is based on your "net income." You may want your accountant to help you plan for the tax liability which might result from making millions.

An example of a trial balance with adjusting entries is shown at the end of this chapter at page 56. This will help to show you the relationship among the trial balance, the adjust entries, and the balance sheet and income statement items.

THE BALANCE SHEET

You have already seen your accounts presented in terms of debits and credits. The Balance Sheet shows your assets (things you own) and your liabilities (things you owe) as of a certain date. Assets are generally your resources and commonly include cash, accounts receivable, inventory, computers, customer lists, furniture, and vehicles. Liabilities are existing debts and obligations such as the loan you established to acquire furniture and equipment, or the amount you owe someone when you bought their existing business.

In reviewing the following example, you might notice your accounting theory at work. DEBITS = CREDITS, and secondly, ASSETS = LIABILITIES + EQUITY. If you are keeping your own books, you should make sure that you prepare a balance sheet. There are actually many bookkeepers and accountants who do not prepare the balance sheet for their clients. This financial statement is an actual snapshot of how your business is doing. It will give you balances of your cash and resources available as well as the balances of all the debts you owe to others. This is very important information to keep in mind when trying to run your business. Don't make the mistake of only looking at just your "profit and loss" statement.

Here is our previous example:

Corena's Chicken Company
Balance Sheet
As of Dec. 31, 1999

	Debits	*Credits*
Assets		
Cash	$ (70.00)	
Accts Receivable	$1,000.00	
Inventory—Chickens	800.00	
Tractor	$6,000.00	
TOTAL ASSETS	$7,730.00	
Liabilities		
Bank Loan payable		$5,500.00
Equity		
Owner's initial contribution		$3,125.00
Owner's draws		(1,000.00)
Income from business		
(increases owner's equity)		**$ 105.00**
TOTAL LIABILITIES AND OWNER'S EQUITY		$7,730.00

The difference between your assets and your liabilities belongs to you, the owner, and is often called the owner's equity or stockholder's equity. A more ancient phrase is called the "net worth." Remember the basic accounting equation looks like this:

ASSETS   =   LIABILITIES + OWNER'S EQUITY
(normally debits)   (both of these are normally credits)

Since you are recording all of your business activity in terms of equal transactions (i.e., left = right; debit = credit) your balance sheet should always balance. The assets should always equal the liabilities plus the equity. Keep in mind that the liabilities are the "claims" of all of your creditors, business suppliers, lenders, etc. You might want to think of the owner's equity in terms of the owner's "claim" against the business. It is sometimes called the "residual equity" because the claims of creditors take precedence over the claims of the owner. If all assets were sold and liquidated, and all creditors (liabilities) were paid, the amount on which you would have "claim" would be the leftover (residual).

Sometimes an owner may withdraw cash from the company for personal use. This withdrawal obviously reduces the assets (i.e., cash) and your owner's equity (the amount on which you would have had a "claim").

When liabilities exceed your assets, you will have to personally put money into your company or borrow funds. There is no residual at this point, and your owner's equity would reflect a negative number. For example:

ASSETS	=	LIABILITIES	+	OWNER'S EQUITY
Cash	=	Debts	+	Equity
$10,000	=	$15,000	+	($5,000)

A negative because you would have to put cash in to pay the liabilities.

A summary of the items which affect your owner's equity is as follows:

Items which **Decrease Owner's Equity** *(recorded as a debit)*	Items which **Increase Owner's Equity** *(recorded as a credit)*
Withdrawals by owner Expenses	Investments by owner Revenues

THE INCOME STATEMENT

Your "net" income is reflected on the Income Statement which shows your revenue and expenses for a certain period of time (such as a month or year). This financial statement is also referred to as the "profit and loss statement." Revenues are often in the form of sales, fees, commission, rents, etc.

Expenses are the cost of services or goods consumed in the process of making the revenue such as materials, telephone, wages, etc. Expenses deplete your assets and decrease the owner's equity in the business. A list of some possible business expenses are listed in Chapter 7 at page 117.

Net income results when your revenue is greater than your expenses. A net loss occurs when you spend more than you make. As you can see, the net bottom line, whether profit or loss, will impact your owner's equity account.

Your accounts have already been present in terms of debits and credits on the trial balance. They are now shown in terms of an "Income Statement." You may note that the bottom line "net income" becomes the figure in the equity section of your balance sheet which makes it balance.

Corena's Chicken Company
Income Statement
For the period ending Dec. 31, 1999

	Debits	**Credits**
Sales		$550.00
Cost of Sales:		
Chicken Feed	$100.00	
Packaging Expense	$ 20.00	
Total Cost of Sales	$120.00	
Gross profit (Sales less cost of sales give you credit balance of $430)		$430.00
Expenses:		
Rent	$300.00	
Telephone	$ 25.00	
Total Expenses	$325.00	
NET INCOME	**$105.00**	
(gross profit less expenses)		

ACCOUNTING PROOF:		
TOTAL DEBITS (Expn and Net Income) ($100 + $20 + $300 + $25 + $105)	$550.00	
TOTAL CREDITS BALANCE (the sales figure $550)		$550.00

You should review the following checklist which will assist you in preparing the financial statements. There is also an additional example of how to reconcile your bank statement, make adjusting entries, and analyze your trial balance if it doesn't "balance."

CHECKLIST: STEPS IN RECORDING YOUR ACCOUNTING DATA

Action Item	Date Accomplished
1. DAILY–Analyze your transactions to identify accounts involved and determine whether or not a debit or credit is required. Code items with the appropriate "chart of account" number.	
2. DAILY–Make journal entries to the appropriate journal.	
3. DAILY–Post the journal entry to the General Ledger.	
4. MONTHLY–Prepare your Trial Balance from the ending balances in your General Ledger.	
5. MONTHLY–Analyze the ending balance on your Trial Balance.	
6. MONTHLY–Make sure your cash account matches your bank reconciliation. Make sure other accounts match your actual amounts. Look at inventory, Accts Receivable, Accts Payable.	
7. MONTHLY–Make any adjusting entry as needed by posting entries to appropriate general ledger sheets.	
8. MONTHLY–Reprint or redo your Trial Balance.	
9. MONTHLY–If computerized, make sure to print the following reports:	
Cash receipts journal or listing	
Cash Disbursement journal or listing	

Action Item	**Date Accomplished**
Accounts Receivable journal (with aging report)	
Accounts Payable journal or listing	
Payroll journal or summary	
A detailed general ledger report	
A detailed trial balance	
Make sure your reports are for the month (such as 6/1/99–6/30/99) and not some strange period. Many computers will assume your ending date is the date you are sitting in front of the computer. Don't let your computer do this or the result might be 6/1/99–7/12/99.	
10. MONTHLY–Prepare your financial statements to include your Balance Sheet and Income Statement.	

BANK RECONCILIATION

Brand New Company
Bank Reconciliation
Dec. 31, 1999

Step 1

Cash balance **per bank statement**		$8,824.37
Add:	Deposits in transit (deposits made to your accounting records but bank didn't get before end of month)	$2,000.00
Less:	Outstanding checks (checks listed in your accounting records but didn't clear the bank before the end of the month)	
	No. 547	(250.00)
	No. 555	(7.50)
	No. 557	(125.75)
Adjusted cash balance per bank		**$10,441.12**

Step 2

Cash balance **per your trial balance**		$10,494.12
Add:	error in recording check #543 computer entry was for $210.00 actually cleared bank for $120.00	+ 90.00*
Less:	NSF charges	(18.00)*
	bank charges	(9.00)*
	Automatic health insurance withdrawn from checking account and not yet recorded on books	(116.00)*
Adjusted cash balance per books		**$10,441.12**

*You will need to make adjusting journal entries in your accounting records to adjust your ending trial balance to the correct/accurate amount.

ADJUSTING JOURNAL ENTRIES (AJEs) TO ADJUST CASH BALANCE TO BANK RECONCILIATION

Date	Account Title/ Explanation	Ref	Debit	Credit
12/31/99	Cash account	**AJE 01**	$ 90.00	
	Telephone expense			$ 90.00

To adjust error when recording check #543 to Pacific Bell. Check was for $120.00 data entry showed $210.00

12/31/99	Bank charges—NSF	**AJE 02**	$ 18.00	
	Bank charges—regular		$ 9.00	
	Cash		$ 27.00	

To record bank charges for December

12/31/99	Health insurance	**AJE 03**	$116.00	
	Cash		$116.00	

To record health insurance payment automatically withdrawn from checking account

Pioneer Advertising Agency
Work Sheet
For the Month Ended October 31, 1993

Account Titles	Trial Balance Dr.	Cr.	Adjustments Dr.	Cr.	Adjusted Trial Balance Dr.	Cr.	Income Statement Dr.	Cr.	Balance Sheet Dr.	Cr.
Cash	15,200				15,200				15,200	
Advertising	2,500			1,500	1,000				1,000	
Prepaid Insurance	600			50	550				550	
Office Equipment	5,000				5,000				5,000	
Notes Payable		5,000				5,000				5,000
Accounts Payable		2,500				2,500				2,500
Unearned Fees		1,200	400			800				800
C.R. Byrd, Capital		10,000				10,000				10,000
C.R. Byrd, Drawing	500				500				500	
Fees Earned		10,000		400		10,600		10,600		
				200						
Salaries Expense	4,000		1,200		5,200		5,200			
Rent Expense	900			900		900				
Totals	28,700	28,700								

	Adjustments Dr.	Adjustments Cr.	Adj. Trial Balance Dr.	Adj. Trial Balance Cr.	Income Statement Dr.	Income Statement Cr.	Balance Sheet Dr.	Balance Sheet Cr.
Advertising Supplies Expense	1,500		1,500		1,500			
Insurance Expense	50		50		50			
Accum. Depreciation—Office Equipment		40		40				40
Depreciation Expense	40		40		40			
Interest Expense	50		50		50			
Interest Payable		50		50				50
Fees Receivable	200		200				200	
Salaries Payable		1,200		1,200				1,200
Totals	3,440	3,440	30,190	30,190	7,740	10,600	22,450	19,590
Net Income					2,860			2,860
Totals					10,600	10,600	22,450	22,450

What If My Trial Balance Doesn't Balance?

If you are using a computerized accounting system your trial balance should automatically balance. This is because the accounting software program will insist that each of your accounting entries balances before you can go to the next step. Keep in mind that this doesn't mean your trial balance is free from error. It just means that DEBITS = CREDITS.

In a manual system, however, locating an error can be time-consuming, tedious, and frustrating. The error(s) generally results from mathematical mistakes, incorrect postings, or simply transcribing the data incorrectly.

If you have a trial balance that doesn't balance, you should first determine the amount of the difference. After you know this amount, finding the location of the error may be easier with the following steps.

1. If the error is $1, $100, $1000, re-add the trial balance columns and re-compute the account balances. You have made a math error.

2. If your difference is divisible by nine, it is a "transposition error." You have had a moment of dsylexia and reversed the order of your numbers. For example, if your balance was $12 and you added it as $21, you will have a $9 difference. If you have a $90 difference, you should look for the transposition in the hundreds column. An entry of $210 written as $120 creates a $90 difference.

3. Check to see if your difference is divisible by two. If so, scan the trial balance to determine whether a balance equal to half the error has been entered in the wrong column (a debit when it should be a credit).

4. If your difference is not divisible by two or nine, you have more work to do. Since you know your difference, start by scanning your journals to see whether or not an entry has been omitted from the trial balance.

5. If you still haven't found anything, sharpen your pencils and roll up your sleeves. Hopefully you are preparing your trial

balance on a regular basis, and last month your trial balance was fine. You should probably underline the place in your general ledger where each month ends. This way you only need to retrace the activity for a single month (GULP!). All you can do now is start retracing your entries to make sure DEBITS = CREDITS. Look at accounts with high volume or areas that may still confuse you a bit. They are your most likely candidates for error.

September 9, 1998

5

Accounting Theory

There are a variety of accounting issues and theories which cannot be covered within the few pages of this basic book. As a result, the information presented to you is not intended to be all inclusive or provide direct accounting advice to any specific business.

There are some issues that are more complex than the basic receipt and disbursement of cash. If you recognize items in this chapter that might affect your start up business, you should consider the use of a professional accountant to assist you with the establishment of your accounting system and the specific identification of your various accounting and tax issues.

CASH VS. ACCRUAL

Another one of the many decisions to be made when starting a business is whether to keep records on a cash or accrual basis of accounting. The basic premise of accounting is that the method of accounting must clearly reflect income.

The cash basis of accounting is simple. When you receive money it is income, when you spend money it is an expense. The increase in money in "the cigar box" at the end of the month is how much you made. Most small businesses which generate their revenue from the sale of professional or labor hours will be on a cash basis. This is the easiest method of accounting and simplifies your accounting process, assuming it is applicable.

This method of accounting is often justified because a business only has a few receivables or payables and because it is so easy to use. However, from a pure theory standpoint, expenses should be matched against income, and not when the business owner has the funds to pay. Revenue should be recognized when you earn the money and not when your customer gets around to paying it. As a result, the cash basis of accounting is not deemed to be in accordance with Generally Accepted Accounting Principals (GAAP).

Don't be put off by this non-GAAP stuff. As a small business enterprise, the cash basis of accounting is adequate and will provide you with a relatively fair assessment of your financial situation. In fact, if you are an individual and self-employed, in most cases, you must use the cash basis anyway when filing your tax return. This is only mentioned so you understand you are departing from good pure theory.

The accrual basis of accounting recognizes revenue when earned, i.e., when you send out the billing and not when your customer pays it. The expenses are recognized when incurred (i.e., when you become liable for a payment and not when you pay it). The accrual basis offers a more accurate method of accounting than the cash basis. It provides for an accurate matching of the revenue earned and the expenses incurred to generate that revenue. Generally the accrual method is used for businesses with inventory, C-Corporations, partnerships with a C-corporation as a partner, and some trusts.

Please keep in mind that if you have "inventory" at any time during the year, the IRS requires your records to be kept on an "accrual" basis. You do not have a choice. These types of inventory industries include the car mechanic, drapery installer, roofer, or electrician that typically sell and mark-up parts as part of their business. In one court case *Thompson Electric Inc. v. Com-*

missioner (1995) the IRS determined that the electrician must use the accrual method. In this particular case, the electric company did not display supplies to its customer or the public, did not itemize them on bids or invoices, and did not sell materials separately from its service. If you don't choose the "accrual" method, the IRS Commissioner has the authority to change it for you if it is determined that it more clearly reflects your income. In most cases this change will increase your tax liability in the year of the change. What a surprise!

If you are currently using a cash method and think you need to switch, you should definitely talk with a CPA. Changing methods of accounting needs IRS consent and a ton of special forms which need to be filed on a special time-line. A voluntary change in method results in some additional tax. An involuntary change (i.e., the IRS does it for you) usually results in a greater amount of tax. A professional can definitely help you minimize your taxes in this area.

INVENTORY = ASSET

Inventory is defined as goods held for sale or "consumption" in a manufacturing or merchandising business. It includes all finished goods, partly finished goods, raw materials, and supplies which have been acquired for sale to your customers. It also includes items which will physically become part of the merchandise intended for sale.

There are ugly little details when it comes to inventory. Since inventory is an asset, you must accurately maintain the number of your inventory items as well as their individual cost. In our last chapter, Corena sold some chickens to Gary's family. As a result, she has depleted her inventory of chickens. From the accounting stand point, she should know the number of chickens remaining on hand and their initial cost. This becomes complicated by the fact that Corena can't tell her chickens apart. Are the ones in the barn yard the ones she purchased for resale, or are they the home grown hatchlings which cost nothing but rooster and hen time?

Keeping up with inventory is a critical task since it affects both the balance sheet and the income statement. As a balance sheet item, inventories represent a current asset which the business has available for sale. As an income statement item, the cost of the inventory sold must be associated with the revenue from the sale of that inventory. The major objective in accounting for inventories is to match the appropriate costs with related sales revenue. This would be easy if the cost of your inventory never changed. Unfortunately for Corena, the cost of chickens has fluctuated wildly since the last presidential election.

Costing the inventory is complicated because the units on hand have been purchased at different prices. Needless to say, the accounting profession has come up with a variety of solutions. One answer is to use "specific identification" of the units purchased. This method tracks the actual physical flow of the inventory items. This works well for large special order or unique inventory. In Corena's case, this means each chicken would have to be identified separately with its own specific cost. This would be way too impractical. There are other accounting assumptions which follow the flow of inventory costs, such as:

1. first in, first out (FIFO) which means the first inventory items in are the first ones sold
2. last-in, first-out (LIFO) which means the last inventory items in are the first ones sold
3. average cost

There is no accounting requirement that the cost flow assumption be consistent with the physical movement of the goods. This is where the true theory kicks in—the flow of the cost follows an assumption rather than the actual asset. The selection of the appropriate cost flow assumption method must be made by you and your accountant. Once selected it cannot be changed without the IRS's consent. Corena has decided on average cost.

The income statement portion related to inventory is called the costs of good sold. This is usually determined as follows:

Beginning inventory
   (per balance sheet as of 12/1/99)   -0-
Plus inventory items purchased $ 10,000
Less: ending inventory (which will be
   on the balance sheet as of 12/31/99)   (4,500)
Equals ending cost of goods sold
   (which will show on income statement for the month) $ 5,500

CAPITAL ASSETS VS.
EXPENSE AND DEPRECIATION

Capital assets are tangible resources that are used in the operations of the business and are not intended for resale to customers. They are also called plant and equipment or fixed assets. These assets are expected to provide a service to your company for a number of years. The number of useful years is often referred to as the "useful life."

Capital assets are usually subdivided into a variety of classes: land, land improvements, buildings, furniture and equipment, vehicles, computer equipment, and computer software. These assets are recorded on your balance sheet at their original cost. In our previous chapter, Corena purchased a tractor for $6,000. This is an asset which will be reported on her balance sheet.

Accounting theory assumes that an asset's usefulness will decline because of wear and tear. The tractor with 100,000 miles on it will be less useful than the new tractor with only 10 miles. In order to adjust for this wear and tear, assets are "written off" or depreciated over their useful life. Depreciation is the process of allocating the cost of an asset to an expense category based on its useful life. Recording depreciation is done to meet a two-fold purpose: first, to help with valuing the asset; and second, to distribute the cost of the asset over its useful life. Depreciation is a process of cost allocation. It does not value assets.

There are a variety of depreciation methods such as straight-line (an equal amount each year), units of production, declining balance, and sum of the years digits. To make things even more complicated, the IRS does not require you to use the same depreciation method on your financial statements as you do on your tax returns. As a result, large corporations will usually have a financial statement or "book depreciation" and a federal tax return depreciation. To make things even uglier, your state has its own depreciation rules which means you will have a third set of depreciation schedules based on state law.

Because of the complexity and time-consuming process, most small businesses will use the federal depreciation rules for preparing their financial statements. For tax purposes, you can use either the straight-line method or the Modified Accelerated Cost Recover System method (MACRS) which is the result of the Tax Reform Act of 1986. The depreciation expense is usually reported on Federal Form 4562. A sample of the depreciation guidelines and this form follow this chapter.

An assets useful life can be difficult to determine. The IRS has published guidelines listing the commonly expected "useful life" for each asset. Of course, the IRS has changed its mind several times, so if you have been in business over 20 years, you are probably using a variety of depreciation methods. Currently, the commonly accepted useful life of office furniture is seven years. This means Corena can depreciate her $700 desk over a seven-year period. Each year, a portion of the desk is allocated to an expense item and the value of the desk is reduced. If this is done using "straight-line depreciation" her depreciation expense is $700 ÷ 7 years = $100 per year. At the end of seven years, the desk will have a zero value on the books. This doesn't mean the desk has no real value. It could be an antique worth hundreds. It just means, that for accounting/book purposes, the value of the desk is zero.

The entry to record depreciation at the end of year one is made as follows:

Depreciation Expense (shows up as expense on the income statement)	$100.00	
Accumulated Depreciation (shows up on the balance sheet to offset initial cost of desk)		$100.00

If Corena sells the desk for $500, she will have a gain on the sale equal to the sales price less the book value ($500 – "0" =

$500 gain). Remember, Corena has had the tax benefit of writing off the cost of the desk over seven years. Any sales proceeds she receives at the end of year seven is pure profit.

Depreciation is recorded in your general journal, which is then posted to your general ledger, and shows up on your trial balance for verification. When Corena bought her desk, the following entry was made:

Office furniture (asset account)	$700.00	
Cash (asset account)		$700.00

The accumulated depreciation account is not a cash fund. It is merely an account name which represents the total cost that has been "written off" as an expense. Because of the fact that the office furniture is a capital asset, Corena will have an expense item of only $100 in year one, even though she paid $700. In year two, and following, Corena will have an expense item of $100, even though zero dollars were expended. In some regards, depreciation is designed for stretching your equipment write off over a period of years, rather than up front. Actually, this was done intentionally by Congress. Your net income does not fluctuate as much if you must depreciate assets over a period of years. This keeps your tax liability from fluctuating which means Congress has a more even cash flow.

The difficulty for small business owners is to determine whether you have a capital asset or merely a repair. An ordinary repair is an expenditure which maintains the operating efficiency of your asset. Repairs are usually fairly small amounts that occur regularly through the life of the asset such as tune-ups for the tractor, painting of the office, replacing leaking faucets, etc. The difference between a repair and a capital asset is usually a judgment call. One good rule of thumb is to look at the "repair" amount and compare that with your original cost. For example, if the tractor needed to have the engine "repaired" for $2,500, it would be safe to assume that this is really a major improvement that extends the useful life of the tractor. In this situation, it would probably be a capital item. However, if your chicken processing equipment cost $250,000, there could be a strong argument that the $2,500 was merely the "repair" of a broken switch.

This may be a good area to discuss with your accountant. Some firms establish a policy, based on their size and nature of business. They will establish a dollar limit for repairs. Any item under the dollar limit is a repair or expense, any item over the limit is a capital asset. Again, this is going to be a judgment call and it doesn't mean the IRS will agree with you. It make sense, however, that the expense policy for General Motors is going to be very different from that of a small local Chicken Company.

WHAT IS MY TAX YEAR?

Your taxable income is based on your "tax year." Most individuals running a business as a sole proprietor will have tax year that corresponds to the calendar year ending on December 31st. As a result, the first year for many businesses is considered a "short year." However, there are situations in which your tax year might not end in December. This would be defined as a "fiscal year" which is a period of 12 months ending on the last day of any month other than December. For example, a Christmas tree farm or orange orchard are a few businesses that might choose to report their income using this "fiscal method." There are of course always a few corporations who try to find tax savings strategies by using a "fiscal year." As a result, the IRS watches this very closely and has made the application process/procedures for a "fiscal year" rather difficult. **This is definitely an area where you should seek the advice of a tax professional.**

INTERNAL CONTROL

As a new business owner, you may need to ask yourself whether or not your company assets are subject to theft, robbery, or unauthorized use. Internal control consists of the company plan to safeguard assets and enhance the accuracy and reliability of accounting records. An essential element to internal control is the assignment of responsibility to specific individuals—especially the handling of cash and bank deposits. Your next step would be to separate duties. When one employee maintains the accounting records, and another employee maintains the physical custody of the cash, there is less likelihood that there will be misuse of cash. A few internal control procedures that you may want to consider are as follows:

- Documents should be pre-numbered and all documents should be accounted for
- Each document should have an "accounting" copy which is forwarded to the accountant or bookkeeper for timely recording
- You should have a safe or vault to store cash/checks before depositing to the bank
- You should store your company check book in a safe place and account for all checks issued
- Use a bank safety deposit box for important business papers
- Consider a locked warehouse for inventories and fencing company property
- Use a locking storage cabinet for accounting/payroll records
- Computer programs should have a password in order to access accounting files

Form **4562**	**Depreciation and Amortization**	OMB No. 1545-0172
Department of the Treasury Internal Revenue Service (99)	**(Including Information on Listed Property)** ▶ See separate instructions. ▶ Attach this form to your return.	**1996** Attachment Sequence No. **67**

Name(s) shown on return | Identifying number

Business or activity to which this form relates

Part I   Election To Expense Certain Tangible Property (Section 179) (Note: If you have any "listed property," complete Part V before you complete Part I.)

1	Maximum dollar limitation. If an enterprise zone business, see page 2 of the instructions......................	**1**	$17,500
2	Total cost of section 179 property placed in service. See page 2 of the instructions.....................	**2**	
3	Threshold cost of section 179 property before reduction in limitation	**3**	$200,000
4	Reduction in limitation. Subtract line 3 from line 2. If zero or less, enter –0–..........................	**4**	
5	Dollar limitation for tax year. Subtract line 4 from line 1. If zero or less, enter –0–. If married filing separately, see page 2 of the instructions	**5**	

6	**(a)** Description of property	**(b)** Cost (business use only)	**(c)** Elected cost

7	Listed property. Enter amount from line 27 .... **7**		
8	Total elected cost of section 179 property. Add amounts in column (c), lines 6 and 7.....................	**8**	
9	Tentative deduction. Enter the smaller of line 5 or line 8.....................................	**9**	
10	Carryover of disallowed deduction from 1995. See page 2 of the instructions	**10**	
11	Business income limitation. Enter the smaller of business income (not less than zero) or line 5 (see instructions)	**11**	
12	Section 179 expense deduction. Add lines 9 and 10, but do not enter more than line 11......................	**12**	
13	Carryover of disallowed deduction to 1997. Add lines 9 and 10, less line 12 .... ▶ **13**		

Note: Do not use Part II or Part III below for listed property (automobiles, certain other vehicles, cellular telephones, certain computers, or property used for entertainment, recreation, or amusement). Instead, use Part V for listed property.

Part II   MACRS Depreciation For Assets Placed in Service ONLY During Your 1996 Tax Year (Do Not Include Listed Property.)

Section A – General Asset Account Election

14   If you are making the election under section 168(i)(4) to group any assets placed in service during the tax year into one or more general asset accounts, check this box. See page 2 of the instructions... ▶ ☐

Section B – General Depreciation System (GDS) (See page 3 of the instructions.)

(a) Classification of property	**(b)** Month and year placed in service	**(c)** Basis for depreciation (business/investment use only – see instructions)	**(d)** Recovery period	**(e)** Convention	**(f)** Method	**(g)** Depreciation deduction
15a 3-year property						
b 5-year property						
c 7-year property						
d 10-year property						
e 15-year property						
f 20-year property						
g 25-year property			25 yrs		S/L	
h Residential rental property			27.5 yrs	MM	S/L	
			27.5 yrs	MM	S/L	
i Nonresidential real property			39 yrs	MM	S/L	
				MM	S/L	

Section C – Alternative Depreciation System (ADS): (See page 4 of the instructions.)

16a Class life					S/L	
b 12-year			12 yrs		S/L	
c 40-year			40 yrs	MM	S/L	

Part III   Other Depreciation (Do Not Include Listed Property.) (See page 4 of the instructions.)

17	GDS and ADS deductions for assets placed in service in tax years beginning before 1996....................	**17**	
18	Property subject to section 168(f)(1) election.....................................	**18**	
19	ACRS and other depreciation	**19**	

Part IV   Summary (See page 4 of the instructions.)

20	Listed property. Enter amount from line 26	**20**	
21	**Total.** Add deductions on line 12, lines 15 and 16 in column (g), and lines 17 through 20. Enter here and on the appropriate lines of your return. Partnerships & S corporations – see instructions....................	**21**	
22	For assets shown above and placed in service during the current year, enter the portion of the basis attributable to section 263A costs **22**		

KFA   **For Paperwork Reduction Act Notice, see page 1 of the separate instructions.**   Form **4562** (1996)

Part V Listed Property – Automobiles, Certain Other Vehicles, Cellular Telephones, Certain Computers, and Property Used for Entertainment, Recreation, or Amusement

Note: For any vehicle for which you are using the standard mileage rate or deducting lease expense, complete **only** 23a, 23b, columns (a) through (c) of Section A, all of Section B, and Section C if applicable.

Section A – Depreciation and Other Information (Caution: See page 5 of the instructions for limitations for automobiles.)

23a Do you have evidence to support the business/investment use claimed? ☐ Yes ☐ No   23b If "Yes," is the evidence written?   ☐ Yes ☐ No

(a) Type of property (list vehicles first)	(b) Date placed in service	(c) Business/ investment use percentage	(d) Cost or other basis	(e) Basis for depreciation (business/investment use only)	(f) Recovery period	(g) Method/ Convention	(h) Depreciation deduction	(i) Elected section 179 cost
24 Property used more than 50% in a qualified business use (See page 5 of the instructions.):								
25 Property used 50% or less in a qualified business use (See page 5 of the instructions.):								

26 Add amounts in column (h). Enter the total here and on line 20, page 1 . . . . **26**

27 Add amounts in column (i). Enter the total here and on line 7, page 1 . . . . **27**

Section B – Information on Use of Vehicles

Complete this section for vehicles used by a sole proprietor, partner, or other "more than 5% owner," or related person.

If you provided vehicles to your employees, first answer questions in Section C to see if you meet an exception to completing this section for those vehicles.

	(a) Vehicle 1		(b) Vehicle 2		(c) Vehicle 3		(d) Vehicle 4		(e) Vehicle 5		(f) Vehicle 6	
28 Total business/investment miles driven during the year (DO NOT include commuting miles).												
29 Total commuting miles driven during the year												
30 Total other personal (noncommuting) miles driven												
31 Total miles driven during the year. Add lines 28 to 30												
	Yes	No	Yes	No	Yes	No	Yes	No	Yes	No	Yes	No
32 Was the vehicle available for personal use during off-duty hours?												
33 Was the vehicle used primarily by a more than 5% owner or related person?												
34 Is another vehicle available for personal use?												

Section C – Questions for Employers Who Provide Vehicles for Use by Their Employees

Answer these questions to determine if you meet an exception to completing Section B for vehicles used by employees who **are not** more than 5% owners or related persons.

	Yes	No
35 Do you maintain a written policy statement that prohibits all personal use of vehicles, including commuting, by your employees?		
36 Do you maintain a written policy statement that prohibits personal use of vehicles, except commuting, by your employees? See page 6 of the instructions for vehicles used by corporate officers, directors, or 1% or more owners		
37 Do you treat all use of vehicles by employees as personal use?		
38 Do you provide more than five vehicles to your employees, obtain information from your employees about the use of the vehicles, and retain the information received?		
39 Do you meet the requirements concerning qualified automobile demonstration use? See page 6 of the instructions.		

Note: If your answer to 35, 36, 37, 38 or 39 is "Yes," you need not complete Section B for the covered vehicles.

Part VI Amortization

(a) Description of costs	(b) Date amortization begins	(c) Amortizable amount	(d) Code section	(e) Amortization period or percentage	(f) Amortization for this year
40 Amortization of costs that begins during your 1996 tax year:					

41 Amortization of costs that began before 1996 . . . . **41**

42 Total. Enter here and on "Other Deductions" or "Other Expenses" line of your return **42**

INSTRUCTIONS FOR FORM 4562

The following is an oversimplified explanation of how to compute depreciation and fill out Form 4562. For a more detailed explanation, you should call the IRS for their *Form 4562 Depreciation Publication.*

If you look closely at Form 4562, you will notice it is composed of several sections:

Section I— The election to expense or "write off" certain tangible property purchased during the year. You can write off up to $17,500 per year. A new law passed in July 1996 increases this amount every year. It does not include property used less than 50% for business, property held for investment, or property you lease to others. This expense is also limited to your taxable income. If you have a loss, you cannot use the Section 179 expense election.

Section II— This section records the depreciation for the assets you bought in the current year only.

Section III— This section shows the depreciation for the assets you bought before the current year.

Section IV— This is a summary. Note that line #20 shows the amount from Part V.

Section V— This section shows the depreciation for *"listed property."* Listed property generally includes passenger automobiles weighing 6,000 pounds or less, motorcycles, pick-up trucks, photographic equipment, communication equipment, video recording equipment, cellular telephones, and computers. Listed property is usually any property that lends itself to personal use. Corena might easily use a cell phone for personal reasons, where it is unlikely that she would use the chicken feeder for anything but business. It is because of this potential personal use that the IRS watches these items more closely.

Section VI— This section shows amortization. Computer software is amortized in this section over a three-year period.

RECORDKEEPING

Except for the part relating to listed property, the IRS does not require you to submit detailed information with your return on the depreciation of assets. However, the information needed to commute your depreciation deduction (basis, method, etc.) must be part of your permanent records. Because Form 4562 does not provide a method for permanent recordkeeping, you may use a depreciation worksheet (see sample) to assist you in maintaining depreciation records. However, this worksheet is designed only for federal depreciation. Since most states have a different method of depreciation, you should have a separate worksheet for state depreciation.

For federal purposes assets placed in service after 1986 will be depreciated using the Modified Accelerated Cost Recovery System (MACRS). MACRS includes the "General Depreciation System" which has the following three methods:

General Depreciation System—200% declining balance, using the half-year method

General Depreciation System—150% declining balance, using the half-year method

General Depreciation System—straight line, using the mid-month method

CLASSIFYING ASSETS

Once you have decided on a method (say, GDS—200% declining balance), you must now look at the property you bought during the year and sort it into the appropriate classification. You can then refer to the depreciation tables to determine your expense. The classifications are shown on the next page:

3-year property—(a) a race horse that is more than 2 years old at the time it is placed in service and (b) any horse (other than a race horse) that is more than 12 years.

5-year property—(a) automobiles; (b) light general purpose trucks; (c) typewriters, calculators, copiers, duplicating equipment; (d) semi-conductor manufacturing equipment; (e) computers; (f) any Section 1245 property used in connection with research and experimentation; and (g) certain energy property.

7-year property—(a) office furniture and equipment; (b) appliances, carpets, furniture, etc., used in residential rental property; (c) railroad tracks; and (d) items that aren't listed anywhere else.

10-year property—(a) vessels, barges, tugs, water transportation equipment; (b) any single purpose agricultural or horticultural structure (Code Sec. 168(I)(13)); and (c) any tree or vine bearing fruits/nuts.

15-year property—(a) any municipal wastewater treatment plant and (b) telephone distribution plants.

20-year property—any municipal sewers.

EXAMPLE

You purchased a computer for $2,500. This would be a 5-year property. It is also considered listed property since it has the potential for personal use. You use it 100% for business. If you have a profit greater than $2,500 you can do one of two things:

1. elect to expense it—i.e., write off the entire $2,500
   OR
2. multiply the $2,500 x the amount shown for year 1 of a 5-year asset (20%).

   SEE THE DEPRECIATION TABLE ON PAGE 75

for year one = $2,500 @ 20.00% = $500 depreciation expense
for year two = $2,500 @ 32.00% = $800 depreciation expense
for year three = $2,500 @ 19.20% = $480 depreciation expense
for year four = $2,500 @ 11.52% = $288 depreciation expense
for year five = $2,500 @ 11.52% = $288 depreciation expense
for year six = $2,500 @ 5.76% = $144 depreciation expense

TOTAL DEPRECIATION $2,500

Since it is listed property, the depreciation information is shown in Section V. The total is then carried forward to Part IV, Summary.

TABLE A—GENERAL DEPRECIATION SYSTEM

Method: 200% Declining Balance Switching to Straight-Line
Convention: Half-Year

Year	3 Years	5 Years	7 Years	10 Years
1	33.33%	20.00%	14.29%	10.00%
2	44.45%	32.00%	24.49%	18.00%
3	14.81%	19.20%	17.49%	14.40%
4	7.41%	11.52%	12.49%	11.52%
5		11.52%	8.93%	9.22%
6		5.76%	8.92%	7.37%
7			8.93%	6.55%
8			4.46%	6.55%
9				6.55%
10				6.55%
11				3.29%
Total	**100.00%**	**100.00%**	**100.00%**	**100.00%**

Depreciation Worksheet

Description of Property	Date Placed in Service	Cost or Other Basis	Business/ Investment Use %	Section 179 Deduction	Depreciation Prior Years	Basis for Depreciation	Method/ Convention	Recovery Period	Rate or Table %	Depreciation Deduction

6

The Joys of
Hiring Employees

If you have employees, you will have the added joys of contending with a variety of additional reporting requirements and administrative agencies.

> *The work related to payroll compliance is quite cumbersome and complicated. This is truly where many small businesses get themselves into serious trouble.*

Whenever a wage payment is made, you must provide the employee with a statement of gross wages and specific deductions. Keep in mind that the labor code requires that all wages are payable twice during each calendar month (with only a few exceptions). This means payroll calculations and withholding summaries must be done at least twice a month for each employee. Because of the personnel and management time required to operate a payroll system, a business with more than a few employees should consider an outside qualified payroll service. It is usually more time efficient and cost effective. Many banks will provide payroll services for a nominal fee. There are many companies that specialize in providing payroll services to businesses. You may be able to find these listed in your local yellow pages or you can call any local CPA office and ask them for a name of a payroll service company.

Keep in mind that as an employer, you must also know which benefits are and are not taxable. This chapter is not intended to enumerate all these options. At the federal level and most state levels, overtime pay, tips, commissions, benefits, and vacation pay are grouped under the common heading of supplemental wage payments. Flat rate expense account allowances, auto allowances, and disability insurance paid by you (the employer) are also among the items to be included as other compensation on a W-2 Form. It is important that you coordinate this chapter with your state's taxation department for specific details at the state level.

DETERMINING THE EMPLOYEE'S CHECK

The paychecks written to your employees are always net of taxes. **These withheld federal taxes, state taxes, social security and Medicare taxes belong to your employee.** The social security taxes are for the employee's retirement. The federal and state taxes are needed by the employees when they file their tax returns in April.

The federal taxes and state taxes are determined using payroll withholding tables issued by the federal and state governments. There is a different table for single vs. married, and there are different tables for different pay periods of weekly, bi-weekly, semi-weekly, or monthly. The social security and Medicare taxes are determined each year by Congress and are a percentage of the gross wages. **These withholding rates and tables are published each year in the IRS booklet called "Circular E, Employer's Tax Guide." State taxing agencies publish similar booklets.** It is important to consult with your state agency. Several states require State Income Taxes (SIT) and State Disability Insurance (SDI) to be deducted based on gross earnings. However, most states specify a minimum amount of gross earnings before SIT is to be deducted.

Prior to paying your first wages as an employer, you will first need to hire an employee. When hiring an employee, you will need to agree on either an hourly wage or a monthly/annual salary. This should be documented in the employee file. Once you have hired an employee, you should obtain the following documentation from them before they start.

a. Have the employee fill out a Form W-4 (shown on page 89). This will provide you with their correct address and social security number. It will also provide you with the information regarding the tax withholding status needed to calculate their paycheck.

b. Have the employee fill out a Form I-9 (shown on page 90). You will need to see two forms of ID. Make a copy of both pieces of ID and make sure to keep these copies in the employee's file.

Your employee file should also contain any employee evaluations you perform on the employee and any documentation on disciplinary action. In case of a dispute or employee-initiated legal action, actual documentation of events is much better than your memory. Keep in mind that you may have to appear before the Employment Development Department, Labor Board, or judge and jury.

You are now ready to calculate your employee's first check. Keep in mind that the withholding amounts and rates change from year to year. The amounts shown are for example purposes only.

Remember that the amount due to your employee was $400.00 and your employee's net check was only $329.40. *The difference of $70.60 is NOT YOURS.* It belongs to your employee and should be turned over to the various government agencies on behalf of your employee. **As an employer, you should NOT be spending this money.** The IRS likens this to theft and imposes stiff penalties on you personally. Don't try to solve your business cash flow problems by using this money. It is cheaper to go out and borrow money than to "use"

Example: Your employee is paid $10 an hour and worked a 40-hour week. The Form W-4 indicates "S-02" (single and two exemptions). Since you pay weekly, you will look at the weekly withholding tables in the IRS and state booklets. Since your employee is single, you will look to the single chart. Your employee's check will now look something like this:

Total hours worked = 40 hrs @ $10/hr wage rate	
= Gross Wages	$400.00
Less: FITW (Fed. Income Tax Withheld)	
(Use withholding tables as mentioned above)	(33.00)
FICA (Fed Insur. Contribution Act) (6.2% of gross wages	
up to a maximum of $62,700 for 1996)	(24.80)
MEDICARE (1.45% of gross wages)	(5.80)
SITW (State Income Tax Withheld)	
(Use withholding tables)	(2.00)
State Disability Insurance (varies state to state)	(4.00)
City/local taxes (applies to only a few locations in the US)	(1.00)
Total deductions	($70.60)
Net check to employee ($400.00 − $70.60)	$329.40

these trust fund dollars! While "using" the employee funds may solve a short-term cash flow need, the end result is usually disastrous.

You are considered to be the custodian of the employee's funds and must therefore act responsibly. Neither the IRS nor state agencies are lenient or understanding of businesses who do not pay over these withheld funds. They have and use draconian powers to collect unpaid payroll taxes from delinquent businesses. The IRS is not obliged to accept installment payments and based on the experience of the authors it appears the IRS has an unspoken policy to shut down small businesses rather than accept installment payments. Once the doors have closed, and your business fails, you or the managers, or anyone authorized to sign a payroll check, may be personally subject to a monetary penalty which is equal to 100% of the dollars which were not remitted to the government agencies (i.e., the employee's withheld portion).

YOUR PART OF THE PAYROLL TAXES

As an employer, you are responsible for matching the federal FICA and Medicare amounts paid by the employee. Your share of the taxes should be remitted to the taxing authorities together with the amounts withheld from your employee's check.

In the previous example, the employer's payroll tax expense would be $30.60 (FICA of $24.80 and MEDICARE of $5.80).

The amount to be remitted to the IRS on behalf of your employee includes the following:

The FITW which your employee didn't get	$33.00
The FICA which your employee didn't get	$24.80
The MEDICARE which your employee didn't get	$ 5.80
The employer's payroll tax expense which is FICA + MEDICARE	$30.60
Amount to be remitted	$94.20

You are also required to make contributions to the Federal Unemployment Tax plan (FUTA). This liability usually varies depending on your FUTA percentage rate. The FUTA payment is made on the first $7,000 of your employee's earnings. You will need to monitor payroll records so that when an employee's earnings exceed $7,000 you no longer contribute FUTA.

Each state will also assess a payroll tax which should be remitted in a similar manner.

The amount to be remitted to your state agency would be calculated as follows:

The SIT (State Income Taxes) which your employee didn't get	$ 2.00
The State Disability which your employee didn't get	4.00
The employer's payroll tax expense which is usually gross wages times a certain percent (determined by each state)	13.60
Amount to be remitted to your state agency	$ 19.60

DEPOSIT RULES—WHEN AND HOW

Now that you know the amount that needs to be remitted, the next step is to know when and how these deposits are made.

There are two timelines for determining **WHEN** you deposit federal employment and withholding taxes—monthly or semiweekly. The IRS will notify you each November whether you are a "monthly" or "semiweekly" depositor for the upcoming calendar year. They make this determination based on the size of your payroll deposits over a four-quarter lookback period. Once your deposit status has been determined, the status remains the same for an entire calendar year. *If you are a new employer, you are considered a monthly depositor for the first year of business.* The rules are as follows:

Monthly Deposit Schedule—Employers reporting employment taxes of $50,000.00 or less during the lookback period are considered a monthly depositor. Withheld taxes for a calendar month must be deposited on or before the 15th day of the following month. Example—payroll taxes withheld for the full month of February must be deposited on or before the 15th of March.

Semiweekly Deposit Schedule—Employers reporting employment taxes of more than $50,000.00 are considered semiweekly depositors. Under this rule, taxes withheld from wages on

Wednesday, Thursday and Friday—are due by the following Wednesday
All other days are due by the following Friday.

HOW do you make the deposits?? **Keep in mind that the amount to be remitted is not mailed to the IRS. (They got tired of hearing the "check was in the mail.") Instead, deposits are made to your local bank with a Federal Tax Deposit Coupon called Form 8109.** The bank does not have these forms so you will need to order these from the IRS. Make sure to give them plenty of time to get these to you. Some new business owners have actually missed a deposit deadline because they didn't have the deposit coupon. If you do not have a coupon, mail the deposit to the IRS. It is better to make your payment than to do nothing. Although most states follow the federal payment schedules, you should verify this with your state administrative offices.

At the end of each quarter, a quarterly payroll tax return must be prepared and filed. This tax return will reconcile your payments against the amount you actually owe. If done properly, you will have made all of your payments before the quarterly tax returns are actually due.

BASIC FORMS AND REPORTING REQUIREMENTS

Payroll involves lots of forms and reporting requirements. The first batch of forms starts upon the initial hiring of an employee. One of these is the Federal Form I-9 which requires proof of citizenship or a green card. The other is the Form W-4 previously mentioned which indicates the withholding status of each employee. Some states require additional paperwork such as California's Form DE-34 which requires certain employers to report newly hired employees, rehired employees, or employees who return to work after layoff or unpaid leave.

a. *Each Pay Period*—The employer is required to give the employee an accounting for the amount withheld and how the calculation of the net check was made. **The employer must withhold** social security **and** Medicare taxes from the employee. These withheld items, along with the federal income tax withheld, are to be **deposited on behalf of the employee.**

b. *Quarterly*—The employer must file the quarterly payroll tax return Federal Form 941 which shows the wages paid for the quarter and the related payroll taxes withheld. The total amounts withheld (i.e., your tax liability) will be compared to the amounts you have actually paid. If you have not made all of your payments, your quarterly return will show a balance due. This should be paid immediately. Keep in mind that you will be assessed penalties and interest for this late payment. The Form 941 will be mailed to the same IRS office that handles your business tax return. Any balance due will be deposited to your bank. A similar state quarterly wage report must also be filed. If your cumulative FUTA tax liability exceeds $100 at the end of any quarter, you must also remember to remit these funds.

c. *Annually*—The quarterly tax returns are then reconciled on an annual basis. You must also furnish a Form W-2 to each employee by January 31 showing the wages and withheld taxes for the calendar year. A complete set of the W-2s should be mailed to the Social Security Administration, Data Operations Center, Wilkes-Barre, PA 18769 by February 28, along with Form W-3 (Transmittal Form for W-2s). These year-end reports must be filed at the federal and some state levels. Upon request, a W-2 Form must be furnished to a terminated employee within 30 days after the request or the final wage payment is made, whichever is later. You should refer to the book entitled *Managing Your Employees* by George Devine (also in the *Run Your Own Business* series) regarding other employment issues.

TIME TABLE FOR FORMS AND REPORTING REQUIREMENTS

Form Number	Title	Due Date
Upon Hiring		
US Dept of Justice Form I-9	Employment Eligibility Verification	Fill out when you hire new employee. Keep on file.
*State of CA–EDD Form DE-34**	Report of New Employees	Fill out when you hire new employee. Mail to EDD.
Fed Form W-4 *State Form DE-4**	Employee Withholding Allowance	Fill out when you hire new employee. Keep on file.
Quarterly		
Federal Form 941	Employer's Quarterly Federal Tax Return	To IRS Quarterly 30 days after end of Qtr
*State Form DE-6**	Quarterly Wage Report	To EDD Quarterly 30 days after end of Qtr
Annually		
Federal Form W-2	Wages and Tax Statements	To employees by 1/31 (Annually)
Federal Form 1099-R	Distributions from Pensions, Annuities, Retirements or Profit Sharing Plan	To employees by 1/31 (Annually)
Federal Form W-3 with **red** copy of Form W-2	Transmittal Form for W-2s	To Social Security Administration by 2/28 (Annually)
Fed FUTA Form 940	Federal Unemployment	To IRS (Annually)
*State Form DE-7**	Annual Reconciliation Return	To EDD by 2/28 (Annually)

Note: This example is for the state of California. You should prepare a similar checklist for your company. Make sure to call your state taxing agency and replace the California requirements with those of your state.

PAYROLL PROCEDURES CHECKLIST

Task	Date Begun	Date Completed
1. Make employee file. Document hourly rate. Include a copy of Form I-9 and Form W-4. Include any similar state forms.		
2. Call various payroll companies and ask for a cost estimate. Remember it will take you about ½ hour *per employee* if you do this yourself. Can you earn more in one half hour than the payroll company will charge you for one employee?		
If you are determined to do payroll yourself:		
3. Determine gross pay by multiplying the number of hours worked by the hourly rate.		
4. Determine the withholding—using withholding tables and percentages. Don't forget various state requirements for state taxes and state disability.		
5. Write the net checks. Give to employees with a calculation that shows the gross pay, amounts withheld, and net pay.		
6. Calculate the employer's payroll tax expense related to the gross wages.		
7. Remit all withheld taxes and the employer's portion of the payroll tax expense.		
8. Determine how to record the gross wages and payroll taxes expense in your accounting records. This step is the same regardless of whether the payroll is prepared by you or an outside service.		

Personal Allowances Worksheet

A Enter "1" for **yourself** if no one else can claim you as a dependent . . . . **A** _____

B Enter "1" if: { • You are single and have only one job; or
• You are married, have only one job, and your spouse does not work; or   } . . . . **B** _____
• Your wages from a second job or your spouse's wages (or the total of both) are $1,000 or less.

C Enter "1" for your **spouse**. But, you may choose to enter –0– if you are married and have either a working spouse or
more than one job (this may help you avoid having too little tax withheld) . . . . **C** _____

D Enter number of **dependents** (other than your spouse or yourself) you will claim on your tax return . . . . **D** _____

E Enter "1" if you will file as **head of household** on your tax return (see conditions under **Head of Household** above) . . . . **E** _____

F Enter "1" if you have at least $1,500 of **child or dependent care expenses** for which you plan to claim a credit . . . . **F** _____

G Add lines A through F and enter total here. **Note:** This amount may be different from the number of
exemptions you claim on your return . . . . ▶ **G** _____

For accuracy,
do all
worksheets
that apply.
{ • If you plan to **itemize or claim adjustments to income** and want to reduce your withholding, see the Deductions
and Adjustments Worksheet on page 2.

• If you are **single** and have **more than one job** and your combined earnings from all jobs exceed $32,000 OR if
you are **married** and have a **working spouse or more than one job**, and the combined earnings from all jobs exceed
$55,000, see the Two–Earner/Two–Job Worksheet on page 2 if you want to avoid having too little tax withheld.

• If **neither** of the above situations applies, **stop here** and enter the number from line G on line 5 of Form W–4 below.

– – – – – – – – – – – Cut here and give the certificate to your employer. Keep the top portion for your records. – – – – – – – – – – – –

Form **W–4**	**Employee's Withholding Allowance Certificate**	OMB No. 1545–0010
Department of the Treasury Internal Revenue Service	▶ **For Privacy Act and Paperwork reduction Act Notice, see reverse.**	**1997**

1 Type or print your first name and middle initial Last name	**2** Your social security number

Home address (number and street or rural route)	**3** ☐ Single ☐ Married ☐ Married, but withhold at higher Single rate. **Note:** If married, but legally separated, or spouse is a nonresident alien, check the Single box.
City or town, state, and ZIP code	**4** If your last name differs from that on your social security card, check here and call 1–800–772–1213 for a new card . . . . ▶ ☐

5	Total number of allowances you are claiming (from line G above or from the worksheets on page 2 if they apply)	**5**	
6	Additional amount, if any, you want withheld from each paycheck	**6**	$
7	I claim exemption from withholding for 1997 and I certify that I meet **BOTH** of the following conditions for exemption:		

• Last year I had a right to refund of **ALL** Federal income tax withheld because I had **NO** tax liability; **AND**
• This year I expect a refund of **ALL** Federal income tax withheld because I expect to have **NO** tax liability.

If you meet both condition, enter "EXEMPT" here. . . . . ▶ **7**

Under penalties of perjury, I certify that I am entitled to the number of withholding allowances claimed on this certificate or entitled to claim exempt status.

Employee's signature ▶	Date ▶	, 19

8 Employer's name and address (Employer: Complete 8 and 10 only if sending to the IRS)	9 Office code (optional)	10 Employer identification number

U.S. Department of Justice

Immigration and Naturalization Service

OMB No. 115-0136

Employment Eligibility Verification

Please read instructions carefully before completing this form. The instructions must be available during completion of this form. ANTI-DISCRIMINATION NOTICE. It is illegal to discriminate against work eligible individuals. Employers CANNOT specify which document(s) they will accept from an employee. The refusal to hire an individual because of a future expiration date may also constitute illegal discrimination.

Section 1. Employee Information and Verification. To be completed and signed by employee at the time employment begins

Print Name: Last	First	Middle Initial	Maiden Name

Address (Street Name and Number)	Apt. ✦	Date of Birth (month/day/year)

City	State	Zip Code	Social Security ✦

I am aware that federal law provides for imprisonment and/or fines for false statements or use of false documents in connection with the completion of this form.

I attest, under penalty of perjury, that I am (check one of the following):
- ☐ A citizen or national of the United States
- ☐ A Lawful Permanent Resident (Alien ✦ A _____
- ☐ An alien authorized to work until ___/___/___
  (Alien ✦ or Admission ✦ _____

Employee's Signature _____ Date (month/day/year) _____

Preparer and/or Translator Certification. (To be completed and signed if Section 1 is prepared by a person other than the employee.) I attest, under the penalty of perjury, that I have assisted in the completion of this form and that to the best of my knowledge the information is true and correct.

Preparer's/Translator's Signature	Print Name

Address (Street Name and Number, City, State, Zip Code)

Section 2. Employer Review and Verification. To be completed and signed by employer. Examine one document from List A OR examine one document from List B and one from List C as listed on the reverse of this form and record the title number and expiration date, if any, or the documents(s)

	List A	OR	List B	AND	List C
Document title:					
Issuing authority:					
Document ✦:					
Expiration Date (if any):	___/___/___		___/___/___		___/___/___
Document ✦:					
Expiration Date (if any):	___/___/___				

CERTIFICATION - I attest, under penalty of perjury, that I have examined the document(s) presented by the above-named employee, that the above-listed document(s) appear to be genuine and to relate to the employee named, that the employee began employment on (month/day/year) ___/___/___ and that to the best of my knowledge the employee is eligible to work in the United States. (State employment agencies may omit the date the employee began employment).

Signature of Employer or Authorized Representative	Print Name	Title

Business or Organization Name	Address (Street Name and Number, City, State, Zip Code)	Date (month/day/year)

Section 3. Updating and Reverification. To be completed and signed by employer.

A. New Name (if applicable)	B. Date of rehire (month/day/year)(if applicable)

C. If employee's previous grant of work authorization has expired, provide the information below for the document that establishes current employment eligibility.

Document Title:	Document ✦:	Expiration Date (if any):

I attest, under penalty of perjury, that to the best of my knowledge, this employee is eligible to work in the United States, and if the employee presented document(s), the document(s) I have examined appear to be genuine and to relate to the individual.

Signature of Employer or Authorized Representative	Date (month, day, year)

Form I-9 Rev. 11-21-91) N

7

Employee vs. Independent Contractor

This section is primarily for businesses who are considering hiring an employee or an independent contractor. It is important to know the distinctions between the two, as well as the resulting reporting requirements.

The employer needs to be concerned whether or not the hired help has been properly classified as an "employee" or an "independent contractor."

If you are hiring employees, refer to Chapter 6. If you have been hired as an independent contractor, you may want to read this section just to be aware of requirements placed on your "employer," however, your only responsibility is the related tax as a self-employed person as discussed in Chapter 8.

Generally, your business will have far fewer obligations concerning independent contractors. You will not have to withhold income taxes, social security taxes, or Medicare taxes. If the total payments to any of your independent contractors is more than $600.00, and your contractor is not a corporation, you must report these payments to the IRS by issuing a Form 1099-MISC. These Form 1099s are provided to both the Internal Revenue Service and the recipient/contractor.

WHAT PAYMENTS ARE REPORTED ON FORM 1099?

Payments of $10 or more, relating to interest, stock dividends or distributions, royalties, unemployment compensation, and state tax refunds.

Payments of $600 or more for **"non-employee" services,** rent, providers of health and medical services, liquidation distributions, or crop insurance proceeds. **(If you are the independent contractor, both you and the IRS will receive notification of the amount you earned.)**

Payments (regardless of amount) for acquisition or abandonment of property secured for debt, broker or barter transactions, fishing boat proceeds, pension distributions, sale or exchange of real estate, and distributions from an IRA.

Payments on construction loans will be reported by banks and escrow accounts effective January 1, 1995.

Payments made to corporations (other than medical/health services) are not reportable and do NOT require a Form 1099.

WHAT IS AN INDEPENDENT CONTRACTOR?

As an employer, you have the right to "control" and "direct" the work of your employees. This includes the right to control and direct the work as well as the manner by which it should be accomplished. An independent contractor is a worker who is subject to "control" and "direction," but is not restricted as to the method of how the work should be done.

You need to be concerned whether or not your hired help has been properly classified as an "employee" or an "independent contractor." Unfortunately, there are a variety of agencies participating in this process and they don't follow the same set of rules. Merely having a signed statement saying someone is a contractor may not be enough to convince the IRS, the Employment Development Department, or other agencies such as the Dept. of Immigration and Naturalization, and the U.S. Dept. of Labor.

The most common reason individuals are paid as independent contractors is because businesses want to avoid paying payroll taxes and worker's compensation insurance. Naturally, the taxing authorities know this. A reclassification from "contractor" to "employee" will usually give the government more money. The **key element** for determining whether or not a worker is an independent contractor is **who has the right to control how the work is accomplished.**

The IRS has developed a twenty-factor control test to help determine whether a worker is an employee or an independent contractor (shown at page 98). Once you have reviewed these factors, you will notice they all boil down to questions which focus on the key issue of whether or not you have "control" over your worker.

If you are uncertain about whether or not your worker is an employee or contractor, you can request a ruling from the IRS using Form SS-8 (Determination of Employee Work Status for Purposes of Federal Employment Taxes and Income Tax Withholding). This form should be completed and sent to your IRS District Director. The IRS will then evaluate your answers by using a point/scoring system. There are forty available points (twenty for employee factors and twenty for independent contractor factors). The points for each of these two categories are totaled and compared. The category with the higher score determines the worker's classification. A copy of Form SS-8 follows this section.

Your state employment office or worker's compensation board may have a different set of questions or more stringent factors. Remember, each agency has slightly different requirements. For example, in California, independent contractor regulations are also applicable for worker's compensation issues.

Even though **owners of commercial and rental property** are not liable for payroll taxes **on unlicensed contractors** who perform services on their properties, they **are liable for worker's compensation insurance on independent contractors.** This court ruling is really an eye-opener.

> A rancher in Mono County, California contracted with Mr. Meier, an unlicensed contractor, to construct a bedroom and bath in the attic of his ranch house with a stairway providing access. While working on the job, Mr. Meier fell from a scaffold sustaining a broken neck which rendered him a paraplegic. The California Supreme Court held that Mr. Meier was an employee for worker's compensation purposes. (*State Compensation Insurance Fund v. Compensation Appeals Board and Virgil J. Meier*, 40 Cal. 3d5; 706 p. 2d 1146)

Let's hope the rancher had adequate umbrella or other insurance coverage because this independent contractor should have been covered by the rancher's worker's compensation policy.

WHAT ABOUT WRITTEN AGREEMENTS BETWEEN BUSINESS AND WORKER?

A written agreement between you and your worker may be helpful. It should indicate the reasons why the worker should be classified as an independent contractor and spell out the rights and obligations of each party. You should go through Form SS-8 and rephrase the questions in terms of a statement. For example:

Question #5 rephrased: Contractor must furnish all tools, materials and equipment to perform the services under terms of this agreement.

Question #7 rephrased: Contractor's workplace shall be of his/her own choosing at a site other than Firm's premises.

Your agreement should also indicate that the worker agrees to comply with all the tax laws applicable to a self-employed individual, including the filing of necessary tax returns and the payment of all income taxes. Although the IRS might not agree with the classification of your worker, the fact that the worker has fulfilled all tax obligations may prevent the IRS from pursuing the matter any further.

It is always a good idea to have this agreement examined by an attorney to evaluate its appropriateness under federal and state laws. Remember, a poorly drafted contract may do you more harm than good.

HOW TO FILE A FORM 1099

Generally, information returns must be provided to the contractor by January 31 and to the IRS by February 28 following the year of payment. A 30-day extension may be requested from the IRS by submitting Federal Form 8809 before February 28.

You will need to file Form 1099 with the IRS along with a transmittal (Form 1096). The IRS is now sharing its data base with many state agencies. You should verify with your State Tax Board whether or not you need to file a copy of the Form 1099 at the state level.

The most common mistake made when issuing Form 1099 involves the use of incorrect basic information such as the tax identification number, name, or address. If your information does not match the IRS data base, you will get a nasty letter asking you to clear up the situation. If the recipient is a sole proprietor, you must always furnish their individual name first. **Ask your contractor for their full legal name.** For example:

Margaret Ann Baker
D.B.A. "Ace Computer Co."
Correct Address
Social Security Number or Federal Tax ID Number
(either is O.K.)

The IRS will use a computer to match the first three letters. If you have used "Ann" instead of Margaret, you will receive a notice. The IRS computer cannot match their first three letters of "Mar" with "Ann." The same is true of "William" vs. "Bill," etc.

You must also get a tax identification number (TIN) from each of your contractors, even for "one-time" transactions. The tax identification number will either be a social security number or a federal tax ID number. Either is OK.

The best form to use is the IRS Form W-9 (Request for Taxpayer Identification Number and Certification) which follows this section. It will help you record the recipient's information at the time services are performed or a contract is signed. **You should have it filled out before you actually make a payment to your independent contractor.** This way you will have all the information you need to correctly complete your Form 1099 at year end.

If the independent contractor does not furnish a correct taxpayer identification number or certify that the TIN is correct, you are required to withhold income tax at a 31% rate.

Naturally there are penalties for non-compliance. The law currently allows the IRS to charge you a $50 penalty per each incorrect Form 1099. In addition, the State of California recently issued a warning (in accordance with California Revenue and Taxation Code Section 17299.8)—**"Business deductions taken on your tax return may be disallowed when Forms 1099-Misc. have not been filed to report payments for personal services."** OUCH!!

IS PROPER CLASSIFICATION SUCH A BIG DEAL?

You may think that hiring an independent contractor is easier and cheaper than preparing payroll tax returns or paying additional money for an outside payroll service. However, the cost of misclassifying a worker can really add up.

As the employer, you should have withheld taxes and didn't. You should have remitted these withheld funds to the government and filed payroll tax returns and didn't. Don't let these types of issues create a nightmare for you. Call your CPA early. Here's only a sample of a few of the penalties:

Penalty for Improper Classification	Penalty can be 1.5% of "wages" paid and 20% of the employee's FICA or 3% and 40% if no 1099s were filed.
Penalty for Failure to Deposit	Since your contractor was not on payroll, you didn't withhold taxes. So you couldn't deposit them. There is a penalty on the amount you didn't deposit. 2% for late deposit less than five days, a 5% penalty for a deposit which is five to 15 days late, and a 10% penalty for a deposit which is later than 15 days.
Penalty for Failure to File	Since you didn't classify your worker as an employee, you obviously didn't file quarterly payroll tax returns. There is a 5% penalty for failing to file. The penalty is based on the amount of payroll taxes due. For each month late, there is an additional 5% penalty (not to exceed 25%).

There may also be an additional 100% penalty (equal to the tax not paid) which can be imposed on a "responsible" person for **willfully** failing to withhold and remit taxes. A responsible person is a corporate officer, a partner, or a sole proprietor. In some cases it extends to employees in the position of managing payroll.

This payroll area of your business involves penalties if done incorrectly. You should think through this issue carefully before hiring your first "contractor" (or employee). There are many CPAs which specialize in the start up of new businesses. An hour or two of their time can prevent you from learning the expensive way.

Checklist—Employer vs. Independent Contractor

1. The 20 Factors of the IRS*

a. Questions 1 through 14, 19, and 20 should have as many "no" answers as possible and questions 15 through 18 should have as many "yes" answers as possible to support independent-contractor status.

b.

	Yes	No
1. Does the principal provide instructions to the worker about when, where, and how he or she is to perform the work?		
2. Does the principal provide training to the worker?		
3. Are the services provided by the worker integrated into the principal's business operations?		
4. Must the services be rendered personally by the worker?		
5. Does the principal hire, supervise, and pay assistants to the worker?		
6. Is there a continuing relationship between the principal and the worker?		
7. Does the principal set the work hours and schedule?		
8. Does the worker devote substantially full time to the business of the principal?		
9. Is the work performed on the principal's premises?		
10. Is the worker required to perform the services in an order or sequence set by the principal?		
11. Is the worker required to submit oral or written reports to the principal?		
12. Is the worker paid by the hour, week, or month?		

*Reproduced with permission from "Employee vs. Independent Contractor," published by Spidell Publishing, Inc.

	Yes	No
13. Does the principal pay the business or traveling expenses of the worker?		
14. Does the principal furnish significant tools, materials, and equipment?		
15. Does the worker have a significant investment in facilities?		
16. Can the worker realize a profit or loss as a result of his or her services?		
17. Does the worker provide services for more than one firm at a time?		
18. Does the worker make his or her services available to the general public?		
19. Does the principal have the right to discharge the worker at will?		
20. Can the worker terminate his or her relationship with the principal any time he or she wishes without incurring liability to the principal?		
Number of federal factors supporting independent-contractor status		
Number of federal factors supporting employee status		

2. **Additional California Factors**

   a. All of these questions should have "yes" answers to support independent-contractor status.

   b.

	Yes	No
1. Is the worker engaged in separately established occupation or business?		
2. In this locality, is the work usually done under the direction of the principal without supervision?		

	Yes	No
3. Is skill required in performing the services and accomplishing the desired results?		
4. Do the parties believe they are creating an employer/employee relationship?		
Number of California factors supporting independent-contractor status		
Number of California factors supporting employee status		

3. Weak points in sustaining independent-contractor status:

_____

_____

_____

_____

_____

_____

_____

4. What can be done to strengthen independent-contractor status:

_____

_____

_____

_____

_____

_____

_____

Form **W-9** (Rev. March 1994) Department of the Treasury Internal Revenue Service	**Request for Taxpayer** **Identification Number and Certification**	Give form to the requester. Do NOT send to the IRS.

Please print or type

Name (If joint names, list first and circle the name of the person or entity whose number you enter in Part I below. **See Instructions on page 2 if your name has changed.**)

Business name (Sole proprietors see instructions on page 2.)

Please check appropriate box: ☐ Individual/Sole proprietor ☐ Corporation ☐ Partnership ☐ Other ▶

Address (number, street, and apt. or suite no.)

Requester's name and address (optional)

City, state, and ZIP code

List account number(s) here (optional)

Part I Taxpayer Identification Number (TIN)

Enter your TIN in the appropriate box. For individuals, this is your social security number (SSN). For sole proprietors, see the instructions on page 2. For other entities, it is your employer identification number (EIN). If you do not have a number, see **How To Get a TIN** below.

Note: If the account is in more than one name, see the chart on page 2 for guidelines on whose number to enter.

Social security number

OR

Employer identification number

Part II For Payees Exempt From Backup Withholding (See Exempt Payees and Payments on page 2)

▶

Part III Certification

Under penalties of perjury, I certify that:

1. The number shown on this form is my correct taxpayer identification number (or I am waiting for a number to be issued to me), and

2. I am not subject to backup withholding because: (a) I am exempt from backup withholding, or (b) I have not been notified by the Internal Revenue Service that I am subject to backup withholding as result of a failure to report all interest or dividends, or (c) the IRS has notified me that I am no longer subject to backup withholding.

Certification Instructions. - You must cross out item 2 above if you have been notified by the IRS that you are currently subject to backup withholding because of underreporting interest or dividends on your tax return. For real estate transactions, item **2** does not apply. For mortgage interest paid, the acquistion or abandonment of secured property, cancellation of debt, contributions to an individual retirement arrangement (IRA), and generally payments other than interest and dividends, you are not required to sign the Certification, but you must provide your correct TIN. (Also see **Part III Instructions** on page 2.)

Sign Here	Signature ▶	Date ▶

Form **W-9** (Rev. 3-94)

Form **SS-8** (Rev. July 1996) Department of the Treasury Internal Revenue Service	**Determination of Employee Work Status for Purposes of Federal Employment Taxes and Income Tax Withholding**	OMB No. 1545-0004

Paperwork Reduction Act Notice

We ask for the information on this form to carry out the Internal Revenue laws of the United States. You are required to give us the information. We need it to ensure that you are complying with these laws and to allow us to figure and collect the right amount of tax.

You are not required to provide the information requested on a form that is subject to the Paperwork Reduction Act unless the form displays a valid OMB control number. Books or records relating to a form or its instructions must be retained as long as their contents may become material in the administration of any Internal Revenue law. Generally, tax returns and return information are confidential, as required by Code section 6103.

The time needed to complete and file this form will vary depending on individual circumstances. The estimated average time is: **Recordkeeping,** 34 hr., 55 min.; **Learning about the law or the form,** 12 min.; and **Preparing and sending the form to the IRS,** 46 min. If you have comments concerning the accuracy of these time estimates or suggestions for making this form simpler, we would be happy to hear from you. You can write to the Tax Forms Committee, Western Area Distribution Center, Rancho Cordova, CA 95743-0001. **DO NOT** send the tax form to this address. Instead, see **General Information** for where to file.

Purpose

Employers and workers file Form SS-8 to get a determination as to whether a worker is an employee for purposes of Federal employment taxes and income tax withholding.

General Information

Complete this form carefully. If the firm is completing the form, complete it for **ONE** individual who is representative of the class of workers whose status is in question. If you want a written

determination for more than one class of workers, complete a separate Form SS-8 for one worker from each class whose status is typical of that class. A written determination for any worker will apply to other workers of the same class if the facts are not materially different from those of the worker whose status was ruled upon.

Caution: *Form SS-8 is* **not** *a claim for refund of social security and Medicare taxes or Federal income tax withholding. Also, a determination that an individual is an employee does not necessarily reduce any current or prior tax liability. A worker must file his or her income tax return even if a determination has not been made by the due date of the return.*

Where to file.—In the list below, find the state where your legal residence, principal place of business, office, or agency is located. Send Form SS-8 to the address listed for your location.

Location:	Send to:
Alaska, Arizona, Arkansas, California, Colorado, Hawaii, Idaho, Illinois, Iowa, Kansas, Minnesota, Missouri, Montana, Nebraska, Nevada, New Mexico, North Dakota, Oklahoma, Oregon, South Dakota, Texas, Utah, Washington, Wisconsin, Wyoming	Internal Revenue Service SS-8 Determinations P.O. Box 1230, Stop 4106 AuCC Austin, TX 78767
Alabama, Connecticut, Delaware, District of Columbia, Florida, Georgia, Indiana, Kentucky, Louisiana, Maine, Maryland, Massachusetts, Michigan, Mississippi, New Hampshire, New Jersey, New York, North Carolina, Ohio, Pennsylvania, Rhode Island, South Carolina, Tennessee, Vermont, Virginia, West Virginia, All other locations	Internal Revenue Service SS-8 Determinations Two Lakemont Road Newport, VT 05855-1555

Name of firm (or person) for whom the worker performed services	Name of worker
Address of firm (include street address, apt. or suite no., city, state, and ZIP code)	Address of worker (include street address, apt. or suite no., city, state, and ZIP code)

Trade name		Telephone number (include area code)	Worker's social security number
Telephone number (include area code)	Firm's employer identification number		

Check type of firm for which the work relationship is in question:

☐ Individual ☐ Partnership ☐ Corporation ☐ Other (specify) ▶ _ _ _ _ _ _ _ _ _ _

Important Information Needed to Process Your Request

This form is being completed by: ☐ Firm ☐ Worker

If this form is being completed by the worker, the IRS **must** have your permission to disclose your name to the firm.

Do you object to disclosing your name and the information on this form to the firm? . . . . ☐ Yes ☐ No

If you answer "Yes," the IRS cannot act on your request. **Do not complete the rest of this form unless the IRS asks for it.**

Under section 6110 of the Internal Revenue Code, the information on this form and related file documents will be open to the public if any ruling or determination is made. However, names, addresses, and taxpayer identification numbers will be removed before the information is made public.

Is there any other information you want removed? . . . . ☐ Yes ☐ No

If you check "Yes," we cannot process your request unless you submit a copy of this form and copies of all supporting documents showing, in brackets, the information you want removed. Attach a separate statement showing which specific exemption of section 6110(c) applies to each bracketed part.

Form **SS-8** (Rev. 7-96)

JSA

Form SS-8 (Rev. 7-96)   Page 2

This form is designed to cover many work activities, so some of the questions may not apply to you. **You must answer ALL items or mark them "Unknown" or "Does not apply."** *If you need more space, attach another sheet.*

Total number of workers in this class. (Attach names and addresses. If more than 10 workers, list only 10.) ▶ _____

This information is about services performed by the worker from _____ to _____
(month, day, year)   (month, day, year)

Is the worker still performing services for the firm? . . . . ☐ Yes ☐ No

● If "No," what was the date of termination? ▶ _____
(month, day, year)

1 a Describe the firm's business _____
  b Describe the work done by the worker _____

2 a If the work is done under a written agreement between the firm and the worker, attach a copy.
  b If the agreement is not in writing, describe the terms and conditions of the work arrangement _____

  c If the actual working arrangement differs in any way from the agreement, explain the differences and why they occur _____

3 a Is the worker given training by the firm? . . . . ☐ Yes ☐ No
  ● If "Yes," what kind? _____
  ● How often? _____
  b Is the worker given instructions in the way the work is to be done (exclusive of actual training in 3a)? . . . . ☐ Yes ☐ No
  ● If "Yes", give specific examples. _____
  c Attach samples of any written instructions or procedures.
  d Does the firm have the right to change the methods used by the worker or direct that person on how to do the work? . . . ☐ Yes ☐ No
  ● Explain your answer _____

  ● Does the operation of the firm's business require that the worker be supervised or controlled in the
  performance of the service? . . . . ☐ Yes ☐ No
  ● Explain your answer _____

4 a The firm engages the worker:
  ☐ To perform and complete a particular job only
  ☐ To work at a job for an indefinite period of time
  ☐ Other (explain)
  b Is the worker required to follow a routine or a schedule established by the firm? . . . . ☐ Yes ☐ No
  ● If "Yes," what is the routine or schedule? _____

  c Does the worker report to the firm or its representative? . . . . ☐ Yes ☐ No
  ● If "Yes," How often? _____
  ● For what purpose? _____
  ● In what manner (in person, in writing, by telephone, etc.)? _____
  ● Attach copies of report forms used in reporting to the firm.
  d Does the worker furnish a time record to the firm? . . . . ☐ Yes ☐ No
  ● If "Yes," attach copies of time records.
5 a State the kind and value of tools, equipment, supplies, and materials furnished by:
  ● The firm _____
  ● The worker _____

  b What expenses are incurred by the worker in the performance of services for the firm? _____

  c Does the firm reimburse the worker for any expenses? . . . . ☐ Yes ☐ No
  ● If "Yes," specify the reimbursed expenses _____

Form SS-8 (Rev. 7-96)   Page 3

6a Will the worker perform the services personally? . . . . ☐ Yes ☐ No

b Does the worker have helpers? . . . . ☐ Yes ☐ No
- If "Yes," who hires the helpers? ☐ Firm ☐ Worker
- If the helpers are hired by the worker, is the firm's approval necessary? . . . . ☐ Yes ☐ No
- Who pays the helpers? ☐ Firm ☐ Worker
- If the worker pays the helpers, does the firm repay the worker? . . . . ☐ Yes ☐ No
- Are social security and Medicare taxes and Federal income tax withheld from the helpers' pay? . . . . ☐ Yes ☐ No
- If "Yes," who reports and pays these taxes? ☐ Firm ☐ Worker
- Who reports the helpers' earnings to the Internal Revenue Service? ☐ Firm ☐ Worker
- What services do the helpers perform?

7 At what location are the services performed? ☐ Firm's ☐ Worker's ☐ Other (specify)

8a Type of pay worker receives:
☐ Salary ☐ Commission ☐ Hourly wage ☐ Piecework ☐ Lump sum ☐ Other (specify)

b Does the firm guarantee a minimum amount of pay to the worker? . . . . ☐ Yes ☐ No

c Does the firm allow the worker a drawing account or advances against pay? . . . . ☐ Yes ☐ No
- If "Yes," is the worker paid such advances on a regular basis? . . . . ☐ Yes ☐ No

d How does the worker repay such advances?

9a Is the worker eligible for a pension, bonus, paid vacations, sick pay, etc.? . . . . ☐ Yes ☐ No
- If "Yes," specify

b Does the firm carry worker's compensation insurance on the worker? . . . . ☐ Yes ☐ No

c Does the firm withhold social security and Medicare taxes from amounts paid the worker? . . . . . ☐ Yes ☐ No

d Does the firm withhold Federal income tax from amounts paid the worker? . . . . ☐ Yes ☐ No

e How does the firm report the worker's earnings to the Internal Revenue Service?
☐ Form W-2 ☐ Form 1099-MISC ☐ Does not report ☐ Other (specify)
- Attach a copy.

f Does the firm bond the worker? . . . . ☐ Yes ☐ No

10a Approximately how many hours a day does the worker perform services for the firm?

b Does the firm set hours of work for the worker? . . . . ☐ Yes ☐ No
- If "Yes," what are the worker's set hours? _____ a.m./p.m. to _____ a.m./p.m. (Circle whether a.m. or p.m.)

c Does the worker perform similar services for others? . . . . ☐ Yes ☐ No ☐ Unknown
- If "Yes," are these services performed on a daily basis for other firms? . . . . ☐ Yes ☐ No ☐ Unknown
- Percentage of time spent in performing these services for:
- This firm _____ % Other firms _____ % ☐ Unknown
- Does the firm have priority on the worker's time? . . . . ☐ Yes ☐ No
- If "No," explain

d Is the worker prohibited from competing with the firm either while performing services or during any later period? . . . . ☐ Yes ☐ No

11a Can the firm discharge the worker at any time without incurring a liability? . . . . ☐ Yes ☐ No
- If "No," explain

b Can the worker terminate the services at any time without incurring a liability? . . . . ☐ Yes ☐ No
- If "No," expain

12a Does the worker perform services for the firm under:
☐ The firm's business name ☐ The worker's own business name ☐ Other (specify)

b Does the worker advertise or maintain a business listing in the telephone directory, a trade journal, etc.? . . . . ☐ Yes ☐ No ☐ Unknown
- If "Yes," specify

c Does the worker represent himself or herself to the public as being in business to perform the same or similar services? . . . . ☐ Yes ☐ No ☐ Unknown
- If "Yes," how?

d Does the worker have his or her own shop or office? . . . . ☐ Yes ☐ No ☐ Unknown
- If "Yes," where?

e Does the firm represent the worker as an employee of the firm to its customers? . . . . ☐ Yes ☐ No
- If "No," how is the worker represented?

f How did the firm learn of the worker's services?

13 Is a license necessary for the work? . . . . ☐ Yes ☐ No ☐ Unknown
- If "Yes," what kind of license is required?
- Who issues the license?
- Who pays the license fee?

14 Does the worker have a financial investment in a business related to the services performed? . . . . [ ] **Yes** [ ] **No** [ ] **Unknown**
● If "Yes," specify and give amount of the investment

15 Can the worker incur a loss in the performance of the service for the firm? . . . . [ ] **Yes** [ ] **No**
● If "Yes," how?

16 a Has any other government agency ruled on the status of the firm's workers? . . . . [ ] **Yes** [ ] **No**
● If "Yes," attach a copy of the ruling.

b Is the same issue being considered by any IRS office in connection with the audit of the worker's tax return or the firm's tax return, or has it been considered recently? . . . . [ ] **Yes** [ ] **No**
● If "Yes," for which year(s)?

17 Does the worker assemble or process a product at home or away from the firm's place of business? [ ] **Yes** [ ] **No**
● If "Yes," who furnishes materials or goods used by the worker? [ ] Firm [ ] Worker [ ] Other
● Is the worker furnished a pattern or given instructions to follow in making the product? . . . . [ ] **Yes** [ ] **No**
● Is the worker required to return the finished product to the firm or to someone designated by the firm? . . . [ ] **Yes** [ ] **No**

18 Attach a detailed explanation of any other reason why you believe the worker is an employee or an independent contractor.

Answer items 19a through o only if the worker is a salesperson or provides a service directly to customers.

19 a Are leads to prospective customers furnished by the firm? . . . . [ ] **Yes** [ ] **No** [ ] **Does not apply**
b Is the worker required to pursue or report on leads? . . . . [ ] **Yes** [ ] **No** [ ] **Does not apply**
c Is the worker requried to adhere to prices, terms, and conditions of sale established by the firm? . . . . [ ] **Yes** [ ] **No**
d Are orders submitted to and subject to approval by the firm? . . . . [ ] **Yes** [ ] **No**
e Is the worker expected to attend sales meetings? . . . . [ ] **Yes** [ ] **No**
● If "Yes," is the worker subject to any kind of penalty for failing to attend? . . . . [ ] **Yes** [ ] **No**
f Does the firm assign a specific territory to the worker? . . . . [ ] **Yes** [ ] **No**
g Whom does the customer pay? [ ] Firm [ ] Worker
● If worker, does the worker remit the total amount to the firm? . . . . [ ] **Yes** [ ] **No**
h Does the worker sell a consumer product in a home or establishment other than a permanent retail establishment? . . . . [ ] **Yes** [ ] **No**
i List the products and/or services distributed by the worker, such as meat, vegetables, fruit, bakery products, beverages (other than milk), or laundry or dry cleaning services. If more than one type of product and/or service is distributed, specify the principal one
j Did the firm or another person assign the route or territory and a list of customers to the worker? . . . . [ ] **Yes** [ ] **No**
● If "Yes," enter the name and job title of the person who made the assignment
k Did the worker pay the firm or person for the privilege of serving customers on the route or in the territory? . . . [ ] **Yes** [ ] **No**
● If "Yes," how much did the worker pay (not including any amount paid for a truck or racks, etc.)? $
● What factors were considered in determining the value of the route or territory?
l How are new customers obtained by the worker? Explain fully, showing whether the new customers called the firm for service, were solicited by the worker, or both
m Does the worker sell life insurance? . . . . [ ] **Yes** [ ] **No**
● If "Yes," is the selling of life insurance or annuity contracts for the firm the worker's entire business activity? . . . . [ ] **Yes** [ ] **No**
● If "No," list the other business activities and the amount of time spent on them
n Does the worker sell other types of insurance for the firm? . . . . [ ] **Yes** [ ] **No**
● If "Yes," state the percentage of the worker's total working time spent in selling other types of insurance . . . . %
● At the time the contract was entered into between the firm and the worker, was it their intention that the worker sell life insurance for the firm: [ ] on a full-time basis [ ] on a part-time basis
● State the manner in which the intention was expressed
o Is the worker a traveling or city salesperson? . . . . [ ] **Yes** [ ] **No**
● If "Yes," from whom does the worker principally solicit orders for the firm?
● If the worker solicits orders from wholesalers, retailers, contractors, or operators of hotels, restaurants, or other similar establishments, specify the percentage of the worker's time spent in the solicitation . . . . %
● Is the merchandise purchased by the customers for resale or for use in their business operations? If used by the customers in their business operations, describe the merchandise and state whether it is equipment installed on their premises or a consumable supply

Under penalties of perjury, I declare that I have examined this request, including accompanying documents, and to the best of my knowledge and belief, the facts presented are true, correct, and complete.

Signature ▶   Title ▶   Date ▶

If the firm is completing this form, an officer or member of the firm must sign it. If the worker is completing this form, the worker must sign it. If the worker wants a written determination about services performed for two or more firms, a separate form must be completed and signed for each firm. Additional copies of this form may be obtained by calling 1-800-TAX-FORM (1-800-829-3676).

DO NOT STAPLE   6 9 6 9

Form **1096**	Annual Summary and Transmittal of	OMB No. 1545-0108
Department of the Treasury Internal Revenue Service	U.S. Information Returns	1996

ATTACH IRS LABEL HERE

FILER'S name

Street address (including room or suite number)

City, state, and ZIP code

If you are not using a preprinted label, enter in box 1 or 2 below the identification number you used as the filer on the information returns being transmitted. Do not fill in both boxes 1 and 2.	Name of person to contact if the IRS needs more information	For Official Use Only
	Telephone number ( )	

1 Employer identification number	2 Social security number	3 Total number of forms	4 Federal income tax withheld $ $	5 Total amount reported with this Form 1096

Enter an "X" in only one box below to indicate the type of form being filed.   If this is your FINAL return, enter an "X" here . ▶

W-2G 32	1098 81	1099-A 80	1099-B 79	1099-C 85	1099-DIV 91	1099-G 86	1099-INT 92	1099-MISC 95	1099-OID 96	1099-PATR 97	1099-R 98	1099-S 75	5498 28

Please return this entire page to the Internal Revenue Service. Photocopies are NOT acceptable.

Under penalties of perjury, I declare that I have examined this return and accompanying documents, and, to the best of my knowledge and belief, they are true, correct, and complete.

Signature ▶

Title ▶   Date ▶

For more information and the Paperwork Reduction Act Notice, see the Instructions for Forms 1099, 1098, 5498, and W-2G.   Form **1096** (1996)

This is not a reproducible form. For information only. Do not file.

9595 ☐ VOID ☐ CORRECTED

PAYER'S name, street address, city, state, and ZIP code	1 Rents $	OMB No. 1545-0115	
	2 Royalties $	19**96**	**Miscellaneous Income**
	3 Other income $	Form **1099-MISC**	
PAYER'S Federal identification number	RECIPIENT'S identification number	4 Federal income tax withheld $	5 Fishing boat proceeds $	**Copy A**
RECIPIENT'S name		6 Medical and health care payments $	7 Nonemployee compensation $	**For Internal Revenue Service Center**
Street address (including apt. no.)		8 Substitute payments in lieu of dividends or interest $	9 Payer made direct sales of $5,000 or more of consumer products to a buyer (recipient) for resale ► ☐	**File with Form 1096.** For Paperwork Reduction Act Notice and
City, state, and ZIP code		10 Crop insurance proceeds $	11 State income tax withheld $	instructions for completing this form,
Account number (optional)	2nd TIN Not. ☐	12 State/Payer's state number		see **Instructions for Forms 1099, 1098, 5498, and W-2G.**

Form **1099-MISC**   41-1628061   Department of the Treasury - Internal Revenue Service

Do NOT Cut or Separate Forms on This Page

9595 ☐ VOID ☐ CORRECTED

PAYER'S name, street address, city, state, and ZIP code	1 Rents $	OMB No. 1545-0115	
	2 Royalties $	19**96**	**Miscellaneous Income**
	3 Other income $	Form **1099-MISC**	
PAYER'S Federal identification number	RECIPIENT'S identification number	4 Federal income tax withheld $	5 Fishing boat proceeds $	**Copy A**
RECIPIENT'S name		6 Medical and health care payments $	7 Nonemployee compensation $	**For Internal Revenue Service Center**
Street address (including apt. no.)		8 Substitute payments in lieu of dividends or interest $	9 Payer made direct sales of $5,000 or more of consumer products to a buyer (recipient) for resale ► ☐	**File with Form 1096.** For Paperwork Reduction Act Notice and
City, state, and ZIP code		10 Crop insurance proceeds $	11 State income tax withheld $	instructions for completing this form,
Account number (optional)	2nd TIN Not. ☐	12 State/Payer's state number		see **Instructions for Forms 1099, 1098, 5498, and W-2G.**

Form **1099-MISC**   41-1628061   Department of the Treasury - Internal Revenue Service

Do NOT Cut or Separate Forms on This Page

9595 ☐ VOID ☐ CORRECTED

PAYER'S name, street address, city, state, and ZIP code	1 Rents $	OMB No. 1545-0115	
	2 Royalties $	19**96**	**Miscellaneous Income**
	3 Other income $	Form **1099-MISC**	
PAYER'S Federal identification number	RECIPIENT'S identification number	4 Federal income tax withheld $	5 Fishing boat proceeds $	**Copy A**
RECIPIENT'S name		6 Medical and health care payments $	7 Nonemployee compensation $	**For Internal Revenue Service Center**
Street address (including apt. no.)		8 Substitute payments in lieu of dividends or interest $	9 Payer made direct sales of $5,000 or more of consumer products to a buyer (recipient) for resale ► ☐	**File with Form 1096.** For Paperwork Reduction Act Notice and
City, state, and ZIP code		10 Crop insurance proceeds $	11 State income tax withheld $	instructions for completing this form,
Account number (optional)	2nd TIN Not. ☐	12 State/Payer's state number		see **Instructions for Forms 1099, 1098, 5498, and W-2G.**

Form **1099-MISC**   41-1628061   Department of the Treasury - Internal Revenue Service

8

Taxes

The amount you may save by attempting to tackle your own taxes can be greatly overshadowed by the fact you might miss tax-savings opportunities available to you and your business.

ESTIMATES

If you are receiving income from a W-2, you will hopefully have enough federal taxes withheld to cover your tax liability. However, some income is not subject to the type of withholding that is seen in a W-2 situation. Examples of this type of income include net income from sole proprietorships (Schedule C's), income from partnerships, unemployment compensation, interest, dividends, alimony, rents, gains from the sale of assets, prizes, and awards. Because there is no withholding on this type of income, you are responsible for making an "estimated" tax payment on a quarterly basis. You might also need to make additional "estimates" if the amount of income tax being withheld from your salary or pension is not adequate to cover your total tax liability.

Most general partnerships do not pay tax since the income, expenses, and credits flow through to the individual partner. The partner must include this income when calculating his/her estimated payments.

Corporations are required to pay tax on the net earnings from the business, as well as interest, dividends, gains from sale of assets, etc.

If estimates are underpaid, or not timely paid, both individuals and corporations may be charged with a non-deductible underpayment penalty. Since these estimates are based on forecasted income, the law does allow for several safe-harbors which will protect you from the underpayment penalty. You should consult with your tax accountant as to whether or not you qualify for the safe-harbor rules.

HOW DO I KNOW HOW MUCH I OWE?

The oversimplified version for determining you liability is to consider **all** income less **all** deductions. The calculation and the payment of these estimated taxes should be done on a quarterly "pay-as-you-go" basis. As the year progresses, the amount of guess work or "estimating" will be minimized. Each quarter will provide you with a more accurate picture of your taxable earnings and the anticipated year-end tax liability.

Corporations can merely multiply their net income times the related tax rate. Keep in mind the tax rates are graduated and that this approach is very simplified.

The tax estimate calculation for an individual who is running his/her own business is the result of a three-part process:

1. Add up all your annual income to include interest, wages, rents, and NET Schedule C. If you file jointly with your spouse, you will need to include your spouse's income and tax withholding into this calculation.

The difficulty with this formula is that you don't really know your net annual income ahead of time. Yet you need to have some idea in order to pre-pay via the estimate. One approach is to summarize your earnings through a particular month, say March 31, and then annualize these earnings for a twelve-month period. This can be done by multiplying 3 months of income by 3/12ths. If your income is seasonal, you can be more accurate by using actual numbers for three months and then guestimating the remaining portion of the year. **Remember you will do this for each quarterly estimate** so your guess work becomes less and less as the year goes on.

Subtract any itemized deductions such as mortgage interest, state taxes, and property taxes. Subtract your personal exemptions. The resulting figure is called "taxable income" and should be multiplied by your appropriate tax rate. This provides you with "regular tax." The tax rates range from 15% to 39.6% depending upon your income level and filing status. The tax rate table on page 123 will provide you with an example and estimate of what these ranges and rates are. Keep in mind that these tax rates are adjusted quite regularly by Congress. The tables are provided merely as an example.

2. Multiply your NET Schedule C or partnership income by the social security rate (approximately 15%). **Net means after expenses.** This will give you the amount of "self-employment tax." A copy of Form Schedule C follows this section. This form should be included and filed with your federal individual income tax return (Form 1040). The self-employment tax is calculated on a federal Form SE which also follows this section.

3. **Regular tax and self-employment tax are added together for your total tax liability.** Divide by four and that's your quarterly payment.

WHEN TO MAKE ESTIMATED PAYMENTS

Corporate   Federal Tax Deposit Coupon Form 8109 is deposited with Bank. A state payment is also due for most corporations. Some states impose a minimum tax even if you operate at a loss!

Individual   Federal estimates made with Form 1040ES is mailed to the IRS. State estimates are sent to your local state tax agency. The deposit dates are listed below.

Partnership   No estimates are necessary, but partners should consider the impact this income has on their individual tax returns. The partners should make individual estimates on Form 1040ES as listed below.

Estimates	Individual Due Dates	Corporate Due Dates
1	4/15	3/15
2	6/15	6/15
3	9/15	9/15
4	1/15	12/15

INCOME TAX RETURNS

Each taxable entity has different reporting requirements. Sole proprietorships (i.e., individuals reporting income and expenses on a Schedule C) must file federal Form 1040 and state returns by April 15. Partnerships must file federal Form 1065 and state return by April 15. Corporations (and S-Corporations) must file federal Form 1120/1120-S and state Form 100/100-S by March 15 if the corporate year ends in December. If the corporation is on a fiscal year, it must file by the 15th day of the 3rd month after the end of the tax year. More time can be requested from the IRS, using a special extension request form.

TAX CONSIDERATIONS

Proper tax planning is essential to make the most of the income tax law. It is not a one-time shot right before the return is due, but rather a year-round endeavor. It ensures that there are no surprises when the return is filed. Income tax laws are quite complicated.

There are some areas in which you should definitely seek the help of a qualified tax practitioner. These include a business with an "operating loss." Many small businesses running at losses have failed to utilize these losses to generate potential refunds. Research and development expenses or business energy expenses may also qualify you for credit against your tax liability. Also, there are extremely significant "elections" which need to be made in the first year of a corporate return. A qualified practitioner can help plan how to best utilize these elections.

If you are doing business in more than one state, it is essential that you familiarize yourself with the tax laws and filing requirements of those states. Each state has its own rules and regulations. If you are in non-compliance, you may be barred from doing business in that state.

WHAT'S DEDUCTIBLE?
THE SHORTCUT VERSION

"A taxpayer, whether a corporation, an individual, partnership, trust or estate, generally may deduct from gross income the *ordinary and necessary* expenses of carrying on a trade or business that are paid or incurred in the tax year." (IRS Reg. 1.162-1)

The determination of *ordinary and necessary* is based on facts and circumstances. An expense is *necessary* if it is appropriate and helpful to a business. An expense is *ordinary* if it is common and accepted in a particular business or industry. A sample list of deductible expenses follows this on page 117.

WHAT IS THE RULE FOR
MEALS AND ENTERTAINMENT?

You can entertain customers, clients, suppliers, employees, agents, partners, or professional advisors. The entertainment must be "directly related" to the active conduct of your business or directly "associated" with your trade or business. Your meals and entertainment should include a business discussion which reflects your efforts to obtain income or other business benefits. (Reg. 1.274-2(d))

Entertainment includes entertaining at night clubs, sporting events, theaters, etc. It cannot be lavish or extravagant. The most important issue in deducting meals and entertainment is the proper documentation. You will need to keep records to document: who, what, where, when, and why. This is most easily done by writing this information on your receipt or credit card slip immediately upon payment. It will save you the hassle at tax time of going back through your records or calendar and trying to remember events from the prior year.

Buying lunch or dinner for yourself and/or spouse does not fall within the definition of "entertainment." This expense does not fall within the definition of "entertainment" because you or your spouse are not clients, suppliers, or professional advisors.

WHAT ABOUT AUTO EXPENSES?

There are two approaches to deducting automobile expenses— the *standard mileage rate* **OR** the *actual expenses.* They are distinguished as follows:

1. The standard mileage rate is basically the number of business miles you drive × allowed rate per mile. For 1995 this is 0.30. If you drove 3,000 miles you multiply 3,000 × 0.30 = $900. The $900 can be written off as a business expense as car/auto expenses. No other expenses for auto use are deducted. The 0.30 is deemed to be adequate enough to cover gas, insurance, etc. Obviously this is the easier method, but you must keep track of business miles.

   OR

2. The other approach is to use "actual expenses" such as gas, oil, insurance, repairs, interest, and depreciation. You can only deduct the percentage you used for business. In order to determine this you need to know your total miles driven and your business miles. This will give you the business percentage.

   Example: Total miles driven = 12,000. Of that 9,000 are business miles. This means your business use is 9,000/12,000 =

75%. You can now deduct 75% of your "actual" gas expenses, 75% of your insurance, 75% of repairs, interest, tires, etc., etc.

Generally, once you pick a method for your car, you must stick with it. You can't go switching back and forth (although there is one exception). In both cases you will need to keep track of your business miles. This can be done with a log book or by writing your mileage in your calendar or day timer. Keep in mind that business miles include more than trips to your clients. It also includes trips to the bank, post office, office supply store, and accountant's office.

SHOULD I DEDUCT EXPENSES FOR A HOME OFFICE?

The set of rules for this business deduction can get quite complicated. The home office must be **"used regularly AND exclusively for business."** If your grandmother visits during the year and sleeps on the futon in your home office, you have blown the "exclusive" test. To qualify as a home office you must fit in **one** of the following categories:

1. office is place to meet clients, patients, customers
   or
2. office is separate structure not attached to home
   or
3. office is *principal* place of business for your business

Items #1 and #2 are relatively easy to determine. It becomes more difficult as a home office if you don't meet clients or your don't have a separate structure. Then you must rely on category #3.

Item #3 was tested in court and has become the well-known *Soliman* case. The taxpayer was a doctor who used the office to do billing, follow-up calls, review charts, etc. He did not use the office to meet clients, nor was it a separate structure. The taxpayer deducted the expenses anyway saying it was his "principal" place of business. However, both the IRS and the courts stressed that in order to be the **"principal place" of business, it must be the place where the goods are delivered.** The doctor or building contractor who does work elsewhere (i.e., hospital or someone's home) and uses the office for bids, billing, follow-up calls, etc., cannot write off the home office. The goods and services are delivered at the hospital or construction site. If this is your situation, you cannot write off a home office.

The architect, however, who prepares floor plans in the home office is actually "delivering goods" and can write off home office expenses.

If you fall into one of the previously mentioned categories, you can deduct rent or mortgage interest/taxes, utilities, insurance, and maintenance—times the business % which is based on a square foot ratio. Depreciation can become a tricky factor if you own your home. **This is another one of those areas where you should consult with your accountant.**

CHECKLIST OF DEDUCTIBLE BUSINESS EXPENSES

☐ accounting
☐ advertising
☐ bank charges for business account
☐ bookkeeping fees
☐ books/resource material
☐ computer on-line services if business related
☐ computer supplies
☐ continuing education costs
☐ copying charges
☐ delivery fees
☐ equipment purchased—kept list of dates, amount, descriptions
☐ equipment rent
☐ fax charges
☐ gifts (limit usually $25 per gift)
☐ insurance (other than health)
☐ interest
☐ legal fees related to business
☐ license
☐ miscellaneous
☐ office rent
☐ office supplies
☐ other office expense
☐ postage
☐ printing
☐ profit sharing/retirement plan stuff
☐ property taxes on business equipment
☐ repairs and maintenance
☐ seminars
☐ software—list as separate item
☐ start-up costs—amortize over 60 months

- ☐ stationery costs
- ☐ subscriptions
- ☐ telephone-cellular
- ☐ telephone-regular
- ☐ temporary help
- ☐ travel (can get confusing)
- ☐ utilities
- ☐ wages

SCHEDULE C
(Form 1040)

Department of the Treasury
Internal Revenue Service

Profit or Loss From Business
(Sole Proprietorship)

▶ Partnerships, joint ventures, etc., must file Form 1065.

▶ Attach to Form 1040 or Form 1041.   ▶ See Instructions for Schedule C (Form 1040).

OMB No. 1545-0074

1996

Attachment
Sequence No. **09**

Name of proprietor	Social security number (SSN)

A Principal business or profession, including product or service (see page C-1)	**B** Enter principal business code (from page C-6)▶
C Business name. If no separate business name, leave blank.	**D** Employer ID number (EIN), if any

E Business address (including suite or room no.) ▶ _
  City, town or post office, state, and ZIP code

F Accounting method: **(1)** ☐ Cash   **(2)** ☐ Accrual   **(3)** ☐ Other (specify) ▶ _

G Did you "materially participate" in the operation of this business during 1996? If "No," see page C-2 for limit on losses .... ☐ **Yes** ☐ **No**

H If you started or acquired this business during 1996, check here .... ▶ ☐

Part I   Income

1 Gross receipts or sales. **Caution:** If this income was reported to you on Form W-2 and the "Statutory employee" box on that form was checked, see page C-2 and check here.. ▶ ☐	**1**	
2 Returns and allowances	**2**	
3 Subtract line 2 from line 1	**3**	
4 Cost of goods sold (from line 42 on page 2)..	**4**	
5 **Gross profit.** Subtract line 4 from line 3	**5**	
6 Other income, including Federal and state gasoline or fuel tax credit or refund (see page C-2).....................	**6**	
7 **Gross income.** Add lines 5 and 6 .... ▶	**7**	

Part II   Expenses. Enter expenses for business use of your home **only** on line 30.

8 Advertising	**8**		**19** Pension and profit-sharing plans	**19**	
9 Bad debts from sales or services (see page C-3).......	**9**		**20** Rent or lease (see page C-4):		
10 Car and truck expenses (see page C-3).............	**10**		**a** Vehicles, machinery & equipment.................	**20a**	
			b Other business property.......................	**20b**	
11 Commissions and fees	**11**		**21** Repairs and maintenance	**21**	
12 Depletion	**12**		**22** Supplies (not included in Part III)	**22**	
			23 Taxes and licenses	**23**	
13 Depreciation and section 179 expense deduction (not included in Part III) (see page C-3)......	**13**		**24** Travel, meals, and entertainment:		
			a Travel	**24a**	
14 Employee benefit programs (other than on line 19)........	**14**		**b** Meals and entertainment		
15 Insurance (other than health) ...	**15**		**c** Enter 50% of line 24b subject to limitations (see page C-4).......		
16 Interest:			**d** Subtract line 24c from line 24b	**24d**	
a Mortgage (paid to banks, etc.) ..	**16a**		**25** Utilities	**25**	
b Other	**16b**		**26** Wages (less employment credits).................	**26**	
17 Legal and professional services .	**17**		**27** Other expenses (from line 48 on page 2)........................	**27**	
18 Office expense	**18**				

28 **Total expenses** before expenses for business use of home. Add lines 8 through 27 in columns .... ▶	**28**	
29 Tentative profit (loss). Subtract line 28 from line 7...	**29**	
30 Expenses for business use of your home. Attach Form 8829	**30**	
31 **Net profit or (loss).** Subtract line 30 from line 29.		
• If a profit, enter on **Form 1040, line 12,** and ALSO on **Schedule SE, line 2** (statutory employees, see page C-5). Estates and trusts, enter on Form 1041, line 3. • If a loss, you MUST go on to line 32.	} **31**	

32 If you have a loss, check the box that describes your investment in this activity (see page C-5).

  • If you checked 32a, enter the loss on **Form 1040, line 12,** and ALSO on **Schedule SE, line 2** (statutory employees, see page C-5). Estates and trusts, enter on Form 1041, line 3.

  • If you checked 32b, you MUST attach **Form 6198.**

} **32a** ☐ All investment is at risk.
32b ☐ Some investment is not at risk.

For Paperwork Reduction Act Notice, see Form 1040 instructions.

Schedule C (Form 1040) 1996

Schedule C (Form 1040) 1996   Page **2**

Part III	**Cost of Goods Sold** (see page C-5)

33 Method(s) used to value closing inventory: **a** ☐ Cost   **b** ☐ Lower of cost or market   **c** ☐ Other (attach explanation)

34 Was there any change in determining quantities, costs, or valuations between opening and closing inventory?
If "Yes," attach explanation ....   ☐ **Yes**   ☐ **No**

35 Inventory at beginning of year. If different from last year's closing inventory, attach explanation....................	**35**	
36 Purchases less cost of items withdrawn for personal use...	**36**	
37 Cost of labor. Do not include salary paid to yourself..	**37**	
38 Materials and supplies	**38**	
39 Other costs...	**39**	
40 Add lines 35 through 39	**40**	
41 Inventory at end of year	**41**	
42 **Costs of goods sold.** Subtract line 41 from line 40. Enter the result here and on page 1, line 4	**42**	

Part IV	**Information on Your Vehicle** Complete this part ONLY if you are claiming car or truck expenses on line 10 and are not required to file Form 4562 for this business. See the instructions for line 13 on page C-3 to find out if you must file.

43 When did you place your vehicle in service for business purposes? (month, day, year) ▶ _____

44 Of the total number of miles you drove your vehicle during 1996, enter the number of miles you used your vehicle for:

   a Business _____   **b** Commuting _____   **c** Other _____

45 Do you (or your spouse) have another vehicle available for personal use?....................................   ☐ **Yes**   ☐ **No**

46 Was your vehicle available for use during off–duty hours? ....   ☐ **Yes**   ☐ **No**

47a Do you have evidence to support your deduction?...   ☐ **Yes**   ☐ **No**

   b If "Yes," is the evidence written? ....   ☐ **Yes**   ☐ **No**

Part V	**Other Expenses.** List below business expenses not included on lines 8–26 or line 30.

48 Total other expenses. Enter here and on page 1, line 27	**48**	

SCHEDULE SE (Form 1040) Department of the Treasury Internal Revenue Service	**Self–Employment Tax** ▶ See Instructions for Schedule SE (Form 1040). ▶ **Attach to Form 1040.**	OMB No. 1545–0074 **1996** Attachment Sequence No. **17**

Name of person with **self–employment** income (as shown on Form 1040)	Social security number of person with **self–employment** income ▶	

Who Must File Schedule SE

You must file Schedule SE if:

● You had net earnings from self–employment from **other than** church employee income (line 4 of Short Schedule SE or line 4c of Long Schedule SE) of $400 or more, **OR**

● You had church employee income of $108.28 or more. Income from services you performed as a minister or a member of a religious order **is not** church employee income. See page SE–1.

Note: Even if you had a loss or a small amount of income from self–employment, it may be to your benefit to file Schedule SE and use either "optional method" in Part II of Long Schedule SE. See page SE–3.

Exception: If your only self–employment income was from earnings as a minister, member of a religious order, or Christian Science practitioner, **and** you filed Form 4361 and received IRS approval not to be taxed on those earnings, **do not** file Schedule SE. Instead, write "Exempt–Form 4361" on Form 1040, line 45.

May I Use Short Schedule SE or MUST I Use Long Schedule SE?

```
                          Did you receive wages or tips in 1996?
                     No │                                         │ Yes
 ┌────────────────────────────────────────┐     ┌────────────────────────────────────────┐
 │ Are you a minister, member of a         │     │ Was the total of your wages and tips     │
 │ religious order, or Christian Science   │ Yes │ subject to social security or railroad    │ Yes
 │ practitioner who received IRS approval  │────▶│ retirement tax plus your net earnings    │────▶
 │ not to be taxed on earnings from these  │     │ from self–employment more than $62,700?  │
 │ sources, but you owe self–employment    │     └────────────────────────────────────────┘
 │ tax on other earnings?                  │                     │ No
 └────────────────────────────────────────┘     ┌────────────────────────────────────────┐
                     No                          │ Did you receive tips subject to social    │ Yes
 ┌────────────────────────────────────────┐ Yes │ security or Medicare tax that you did not  │────▶
 │ Are you using one of the optional       │────▶│ report to your employer?                  │
 │ methods to figure your net earnings     │ No  └────────────────────────────────────────┘
 │ (see page SE–3)?                        │◀────
 └────────────────────────────────────────┘
                     No
 ┌────────────────────────────────────────┐ Yes
 │ Did you receive church employee income  │────▶
 │ reported on Form W–2 of $108.28 or more?│
 └────────────────────────────────────────┘
                     No
 ┌────────────────────────────────────────┐     ┌────────────────────────────────────────┐
 │ YOU MAY USE SHORT SCHEDULE SE BELOW     │────▶│ YOU MUST USE LONG SCHEDULE SE ON THE BACK│
 └────────────────────────────────────────┘     └────────────────────────────────────────┘
```

Section A – Short Schedule SE. Caution: Read above to see if you can use Short Schedule SE.

1	Net farm profit or (loss) from Schedule F, line 36, and farm partnerships, Schedule K–1 (Form 1065), line 15a	**1**	
2	Net profit or (loss) from Schedule C, line 31; Schedule C–EZ, line 3; and Schedule K–1 (Form 1065), line 15a (other than farming). Ministers and members of religious orders see page SE–1 for amounts to report on this line. See page SE–2 for other income to report	**2**	
3	Combine lines 1 and 2	**3**	
4	**Net earnings from self–employment.** Multiply line 3 by 92.35% (.9235). If less than $400, **do not** file this schedule; you do not owe self–employment tax . . . . ▶	**4**	
5	**Self–employment tax.** If the amount on line 4 is: ● $62,700 or less, multiply line 4 by 15.3% (.153). Enter the result here and on **Form 1040, line 45.** ● More than $62,700, multiply line 4 by 2.9% (.029). Then, add $7,774.80 to the result. Enter the total here and on **Form 1040, line 45.**	**5**	
6	**Deduction for one–half of self–employment tax.** Multiply line 5 by 50% (.5). Enter the result here and on **Form 1040, line 25** **6**		

For Paperwork Reduction Act Notice, see Form 1040 instructions.   Schedule SE (Form 1040) 1996

Schedule SE (Form 1040) 1996   Attachment Sequence No. **17**   Page **2**

Name of person with **self-employment** income (as shown on Form 1040)	Social security number of person with **self-employment** income. . . . ▶

Section B – Long Schedule SE

Part I Self-Employment Tax

Note: If your only income subject to self-employment tax is **church employee income**, skip lines 1 through 4b. Enter –0– on line 4c and go to line 5a. Income from services you performed as a minister or a member of a religious order **is not** church employee income. See page SE-1.

A If you are a minister, member of a religious order, or Christian Science practitioner **and you** filed Form 4361, but you had $400 or more of **other** net earnings from self-employment, check here and continue with Part I . . . . ▶ ☐

1	Net farm profit or (loss) from Schedule F, line 36, and farm partnerships, Schedule K–1 (Form 1065), line 15a. **Note:** Skip this line if you use the farm optional method. See page SE-3	**1**		
2	Net profit or (loss) from Schedule C, line 31; Schedule C–EZ, line 3; and Schedule K–1 (Form 1065), **line 15a** (other than farming). Ministers and members of religious orders see page SE-1 for amounts to report on this line. See page SE-2 for other income to report. **Note:** Skip this line if you use the nonfarm optional method. See page SE-3	**2**		
3	Combine lines 1 and 2	**3**		
4a	If line 3 is more than zero, multiply line 3 by 92.35% (.9235). Otherwise, enter amount from line 3	**4a**		
b	If you elected one or both of the optional methods, enter the total of lines 15 and 17 here	**4b**		
c	Combine lines 4a and 4b. If less than $400, **do not** file this schedule; you do not owe self-employment tax. **Exception.** If less than $400 and you had **church employee income**, enter –0– and continue . . . . ▶	**4c**		
5a	Enter your **church employee income** from Form W–2. **Caution:** See page SE-1 for definition of church employee income	**5a**		
b	Multiply line 5a by 92.35% (.9235). If less than $100, enter –0–	**5b**		
6	**Net earnings from self-employment.** Add lines 4c and 5b	**6**		
7	Maximum amount of combined wages and self-employment earnings subject to social security tax or the 6.2% portion of the 7.65% railroad retirement (tier 1) tax for 1996	**7**	62,700	00
8a	Total social security wages and tips (total of boxes 3 and 7 on Form(s) W–2) and railroad retirement (tier 1) compensation	**8a**		
b	Unreported tips subject to social security tax (from Form 4137, line 9)	**8b**		
c	Add lines 8a and 8b	**8c**		
9	Subtract line 8c from line 7. If zero or less, enter –0– here and on line 10 and go to line 11 . . . . ▶	**9**		
10	Multiply the **smaller** of line 6 or line 9 by 12.4% (.124)	**10**		
11	Multiply line 6 by 2.9% (.029)	**11**		
12	**Self-employment tax.** Add lines 10 and 11. Enter here and on **Form 1040, line 45**	**12**		
13	**Deduction for one-half of self-employment tax.** Multiply line 12 by 50% (.5). Enter the result here and on **Form 1040, line 25**	**13**		

Part II Optional Methods To Figure Net Earnings (See page SE-3.)

Farm Optional Method. You may use this method **only if:**

● Your gross farm income [1] was not more than $2,400 **or**

● Your gross farm income [1] was more than $2,400 and your net farm profits [2] were less than $1,733.

14	Maximum income for optional methods	**14**	1,600	00
15	Enter the **smaller** of: two-thirds (2/3) of gross farm income [1] (not less than zero) **or** $1,600. Also, include this amount on line 4b above	**15**		

Nonfarm Optional Method. You may use this method **only if:**

● Your net nonfarm profits [3] were less than $1,733 and also less than 72.189% of your gross nonfarm income, [4] **and**

● You had net earnings from self-employment of at least $400 in 2 of the prior 3 years.

Caution: You may use this method no more than five times.

16	Subtract line 15 from line 14	**16**	
17	Enter the **smaller** of: two-thirds (2/3) of gross nonfarm income [4] (not less than zero) **or** the amount on line 16. Also, include this amount on line 4b above	**17**	

[1] From Schedule F, line 11, and Schedule K–1 (Form 1065), line 15b.   [3] From Schedule C, line 31; Schedule C–EZ, line 3; and Schedule K–1 (Form 1065), line 15a.
[2] From Schedule F, line 36, and Schedule K–1 (Form 1065), line 15a.   [4] From Schedule C, line 7; Schedule C–EZ, line 1; and Schedule K–1 (Form 1065), line 15c.

1996 Tax Rate Schedules

*Use **only** if your taxable income (Form 1040, line 37) is $100,000 or more. If less, use the **Tax Table.** Even though you cannot use the Tax Rate Schedules below if your taxable income is less than $100,000, all levels of taxable income are shown so taxpayers can see the tax rate that applies to each level.*

Schedule X—Use if your filing status is **Single**

If the amount on Form 1040, line 37, is: Over—	But not over—	Enter on Form 1040, line 38	of the amount over—
$0	$24,000	.... 15%	$0
24,000	58,150	$3,600.00 + 28%	24,000
58,150	121,300	13,162.00 + 31%	58,150
121,300	263,750	32,738.50 + 36%	121,300
263,750	....	84,020.50 + 39.6%	263,750

Schedule Y-1—Use if your filing status is **Married filing jointly** or **Qualifying widow(er)**

If the amount on Form 1040, line 37, is: Over—	But not over—	Enter on Form 1040, line 38	of the amount over—
$0	$40,100	.... 15%	$0
40,100	96,900	$6,015.00 + 28%	40,100
96,900	147,700	21,919.00 + 31%	96,900
147,700	263,750	37,667.00 + 36%	147,700
263,750	....	79,445.00 + 39.6%	263,750

Schedule Y-2—Use if your filing status is **Married filing separately**

If the amount on Form 1040, line 37, is: Over—	But not over—	Enter on Form 1040, line 38	of the amount over—
$0	$20,050	.... 15%	$0
20,050	48,450	$3,007.50 + 28%	20,050
48,450	73,850	10,959.50 + 31%	48,450
73,850	131,875	18,833.50 + 36%	73,850
131,875	....	39,722.50 + 39.6%	131,875

Schedule Z—Use if your filing status is **Head of household**

If the amount on Form 1040, line 37, is: Over—	But not over—	Enter on Form 1040, line 38	of the amount over—
$0	$32,150	.... 15%	$0
32,150	83,050	$4,822.50 + 28%	32,150
83,050	134,500	19,074.50 + 31%	83,050
134,500	263,750	35,024.00 + 36%	134,500
263,750	....	81,554.00 + 39.6%	263,750

9

Insurance

With the exception of worker's compensation insurance, very little insurance coverage is mandatory. No one likes to pay for insurance, but every business person needs it. Without proper insurance, you could lose all of the money, time, and effort you put into your company. Business insurance comes in a variety of coverages that protect you and your employees from losses you can't afford on your own. Insurance also allows you to continue your business in the face of those losses.

Usually you will want to begin by insuring against risks that could have a significant impact on your business. Your need for business insurance will increase with the success and complexity of your business. You should work with an experienced broker who can help consider your basic risks and evaluate your proposals for coverage. The types and amounts of coverage should be evaluated on a cost-benefit basis just like any other commodity that you purchase. Ask your friends and business colleagues for insurance company referrals before getting started. Remember to check out the reputation of the company that is underwriting the policy. Company ratings should be available through your insurance broker. Most insurance companies are regulated by the State Commissioner of Insurance.

Some of the various insurance coverages are as follows.

WORKER'S COMPENSATION

This insurance is for on-the-job injuries and occupational hazards. In some states, failure to insure is a misdemeanor. If you continue to operate your business without obtaining insurance after a "stop-order" has been issued, you may end up with a fine or jail sentence. All 50 states have different forms of worker's compensation laws.

This is one area in which you must be knowledgeable. In some states it is wise to cover sub-contractors as well as employees. You should establish a habit of securing a copy of your subcontractor's worker's compensation policy before allowing them to perform services for your company. If they do not have a policy, you should add them to your company's policy or look for another sub-contractor.

You may obtain worker's compensation insurance through a private carrier. There are twelve states in which you can purchase this insurance through a competitive state fund called the State Compensation Insurance Fund.

The worker's compensation laws provide the payment of four types of benefits:

1. *Medical benefits*—an injured employee is entitled to receive all medical treatment needed to recover. These medical benefits are provided without limits in every state.
2. *Income benefits*—an injured employee is entitled to income benefits for lost wages. This is based on a medical disability which is either partial or total, temporary or permanent. The benefits are usually paid after three to five days as a benefit for lost wages.
3. *Rehabilitation benefits*—an injured employee is entitled to rehabilitation benefits for an injury which occurred on the job.

The rehabilitation includes therapy vocational training and devices such as artificial limbs.

4. *Death benefits*—A burial allowance is provided in the amount of one to three thousand dollars. Additional death benefits are provided in the form of weekly benefits for a surviving spouse and/or children.

COMMERCIAL CRIME COVERAGE OR FIDELITY BOND

As crime becomes more sophisticated with the use of computers, it has become even more important to protect yourself from employee theft. Your most important control is good internal control. Separation of duties and management involvement is just good business practice.

Before an insurance company will bond you, or issue insurance to cover a loss, they may inspect your company and require you to increase your internal safeguards to protect your property.

Coverage for employee dishonesty is available through insurance or a fidelity bond. Both provide about the same protection.

This insurance covers the risk of loss from theft by employees. If your business deals in large amounts of cash, negotiable securities, or your employees have check-signing authority, you may consider this coverage. Certain industries are required to carry this insurance by regulatory authorities.

Be sure to know the length of your insured period and the limits of the insurer's liability. Are you covered for all employee dishonesty, are there limits per employee or per loss, what is the discovery period?

COMMERCIAL PROPERTY AND CASUALTY INSURANCE

This insurance is for fire, flood, theft, and other hazards involving property and premises such as building, equipment, and cars. Computer coverage is also available; however, you should probably list this separately. An important feature to be aware of is that this insurance should pay for the *"replacement cost"* of your damaged equipment or building. Be wary of the policy that reimburses you for the *"original costs."* Your original cost on that tractor may have been much less than the replacement cost.

Look to insurance package discounts to minimize gaps in coverage and reduce costs. Rating factors are usually reduced when multiple coverages are bundled together in one package.

GENERAL LIABILITY

General liability coverage covers a vast array of exposures. These policies protect you against any legal responsibility occurring from injuries suffered by other people or corporations. Many times these policies seem great, but read the small print. These policies are full of exclusions. Know the exclusions.

Professional Liability Insurance

This is sometimes referred to as "malpractice insurance" and is prudent for every professional in any capacity. Usually each area of professional expertise has its own special insurance resources or companies.

You should obtain such a policy following notification of licenser by your professional State Board. This insurance will protect you against claims and liability suits resulting from your professional services and acts or omissions of employees for whom you are responsible.

These policies' coverages are either "Claims Made" or "Occurrence." The "claims made" policy pays only on claims made during the policy period. An occurrence policy will pay on an occurrence happening during the policy period. You should be familiar with the type of policy you own. You may wish to buy a "tail" on your policy that will cover acts that occurred prior to your policy period but discovered during the current policy period.

Pollution Liability Coverage

Most liability policies exclude pollution. However, if you are moving toxic materials, you may be wise to have a rider put on your policy to cover this pollution and the cleanup cost.

Liquor Liability Coverage

This coverage is used for companies that have incidental exposure to furnishing alcohol to clients or employees. It will not protect you from selling alcohol to minors.

BUSINESS INTERRUPTION

This covers the loss of revenues your business would experience if you were forced to shut down for reasons beyond your control. Some policies extend coverage to include loss through suspension of practice caused by interruption of water or power supplies. While this is obviously a valuable insurance, you should carefully consider the cost of the premiums relative to the profits you might lose during a short shut-down.

DISABILITY INSURANCE

This insurance protects your most valuable assets—your stream of income. It should be purchased as early as possible in your career for two reasons. First, it is the most difficult policy to qualify for physically, so it should be purchased while you are healthy and no pre-existing conditions exist. Second, the younger you are when you purchase the policy, the lower the premiums will be (and remain for the life of the contract). If you do not have any disability insurance, you will have to rely on social security supplements for your disability. Keep in mind that **before you can receive any social security disability payments, you must first be unable to do *ANY* type of work for twelve months.** Without disability income or substantial resources, twelve months with a disability may lead to a financial nightmare.

If you cannot afford the disability insurance quoted by private carriers, check with your State Employment Development Department and ask whether they offer an "elective state disability insurance." Usually it does not require any type of physical and is similar to the "disability insurance" withheld from W-2 employees.

LIFE INSURANCE

Life insurance should be considered when you have someone to support who may not be fully capable of supporting themselves. It should also be considered if you have a substantial amount of business loans which you don't want to leave to your family.

The least expensive type of policy is Term Life (usually less than $1 per year per $1,000 of insurance). It is renewed on an annual basis by simply paying the current premium. In most cases, the policy can be renewed for many years into the future and can be converted to any of the other type of life insurance at a later time.

There are also a variety of other types of life insurance policies to include Whole Life, Universal Life, Ordinary Life, First-to-Die, Second-to-Die, and a combination of all of the above. Each serves a specific purpose and should be discussed with your insurance broker to determine which policy addresses your individual insurance needs.

Life policies can be used as an employee benefit with some beneficial tax benefits. In addition, the business can take out a life policy on key employees. The loss of a key employee can be a very costly event for a business. Loss of talent, the cost to replace, and the training of the replacement are expensive. A life policy to cover this cost can be an effective option.

COMMERCIAL UMBRELLA

You may wish to purchase an umbrella policy to protect against the multi-million-dollar liability lawsuit. The umbrella policy is a policy that insures all your primary policies to a higher limit.

Under an umbrella policy you may be able to secure up to $30 million in additional coverage. The umbrella policy can cover insurance gaps created by oversight or policy design. The umbrella policy may also offer you coverage where no primary insurance exists. Umbrella policies can be quite creative so be careful you are getting the coverage you requested. The best umbrella policies are written by the same firm that is insuring the underlying policies.

SUMMARY

Insurance is a very complex subject. You need to learn enough about the insurance products to make you get the right protection. Utilize your insurance agent wisely. Use the risk evaluation checklist at the end of this chapter to assist you with focusing on your most important needs. Insurance may seem to be an evil cost of doing business when it's not needed; however, it can become your best friend at the time of a disaster or loss.

CHECKLIST FOR INSURANCE COVERAGE ISSUES

Coverage Issues	Date Began	Date Completed
1. If you are licensed by a State Board, inquire as to whether or not your profession requires professional liability insurance. Talk to others in your profession for referrals to specialized insurance companies. Obtain a policy for professional liability.		
2. If you are hiring employees, call your State Development or Employment Department and ask about worker's compensation insurance. The rates might be cheaper than a commercial carrier. Obtain worker's compensation insurance.		
3. Check with your appropriate state agency about obtaining some type of disability insurance coverage. At a minimum you should obtain some type of "elective state disability insurance." Obtain disability insurance.		
4. Talk to an insurance broker about your other insurance needs such as property insurance, business interruption, and life insurance. If you are self-employed, and your spouse has no medical coverage, then health insurance will also be an issue. Do some comparative shopping for the right insurance coverage.		
5. Ask yourself the following questions and do the appropriate research:		

Coverage Issues	Date Began	Date Completed
Is the cost of my insurance policy built into the product being sold?		
Can I reduce my policy costs by better internal controls?		
Does one insurance policy overlap another policy?		
What are the cancellation conditions?		
Can I self-insure part of my business insurance?		
How strong is the insurance company taking my money?		
Did I shop the market place for the best cost? Get three comparisons!		
Have I insured against all risks that would have a significant impact on my business or family?		

CHECKLIST FOR INSURANCE RISK EVALUATION

Use the following checklist to rate the degree of risk your business might have regarding the various types of insurance coverages.

This is a three-step process:

1. Give a numeric rating to the "probability of occurrence." You can give yourself five points, three points, or one point, depending upon your assessment of the "probability."

2. Give yourself a numeric rating to rate the financial impact such a loss would have on you or your family. A significant financial impact would be a 10; moderate, a 5; and little, a 1.

3. Add your figures together to determine your total score. Those with the highest score should be your first areas of concern and coverage.

Type of Risks	Probability of Occurrence				Financial Impact				
	High 5	Average 3	Low 1	+	High 10	Average 5	Low 1	=	TOTAL
1. Loss of Property									
a. Total Loss				+				=	
b. Loss of Use				+				=	
c. Major Repairs				+				=	
2. Loss of Income									
a. Business Interruption				+				=	
b. Owner gets sick				+				=	
c. Owner dies				+				=	
3. Injury to Others									
a. Person				+				=	
b. Property				+				=	
c. Reputation				+				=	
4. Injury to Employees or Owner									
a. Routine Events				+				=	
b. Catastrophic Event				+				=	
c. Age				+				=	
5. Other Occurrences									
a. Professional Liability				+				=	
b. Board of Directors				+				=	
c. Inflation Adjustments				+				=	

10

Balancing the Budget

Budgeting is an integral part of society. Each day we try to budget our time, our meals, our kid's time, and our money. Most of this process is done mentally and never put on paper. Just as families budget time and money, your business must also develop a financial plan. This is called a budget and is a formal written summary of your goals and intentions in terms of dollars.

There are several type of budgets with which you may be familiar such as: the negative Federal Budget, the "try to break-even budget," or the "I'm going to make a profit" budget. Since you have started your own business for the purpose of generating a profit, we will concentrate on this profit motive. **You will now see the significant contribution your accounting information makes to your management process.** Keeping track of the historical data, cost relationships, and various overhead items will help you make the proper management decisions. Accounting will translate your business plans into measurable financial goals.

WHY BUDGET?

Budgeting offers many advantages to your company. It requires that you look at past historical performances by comparing your "actual" revenue and expenses to your "targeted" revenue and expenses. You can then evaluate your accomplishments. Because of this review, budgeting often creates an early warning system for potential problems.

Budgeting also requires you to look ahead and formalize future goals. By establishing a budget, you can set goals for achieving a certain level of income and monitor your expenses. Together the historical review and futuristic focus will aid in the attainment of your business profits. Many small business owners have remarked that their increase in profit margins did not occur until they had a written revenue goal and a method in which to monitor expenses. Other business owners need to know their sales levels in terms of dollars and how hard they need to work to make the budget work. You know you are on top of your business when you can tell your accountant that you need to sell 3.25 items per day in order to make your budget work and meet your financial goals.

Keep in mind that budgeting is an aid to you as the business owner. It is only as good as you want it to be. The more time and effort you spend on your budget, the greater your reward from the budget process.

PREPARING A BUDGET

A budget is a formal written document. The most common budget period is one year, but this can vary depending upon whether or not your business has seasonal or cyclical fluctuations.

The budgeting process usually begins with the collection of accounting data. In order to prepare a strong and achievable budget, you must analyze each item of income and expense from a prior year. If your accounting system is a mess and the figures are inaccurate, the numbers used in your budget will be useless.

If you can review your prior year figures with confidence, try to cultivate your strong areas and look for ways to increase performance or volume. You also need to analyze your weak spots. If possible, set up some type of internal control over the weak areas. A cost analysis will help you determine if you are actually making money on the sale of a certain product. It's amazing how many small business owners do not know if they are making a profit on service, parts, or sales. Others don't know whether they are actually making or losing money on a particular job. The purpose of the accounting and budgetary process is to help you answer these questions and make the right management decisions. You can't plug the leaks in your revenue ship if you don't know where the holes are.

If your business is in its first year, your budget will involve a little more homework. Keep in mind that the budget is an expression of management's goals. Try to determine the number of billable hours you might reasonably expect to charge within a year's time. If you are in sales, try to establish the number of items you could be able to sell. After determining the revenue portion, you should look to your expenses. Obviously, your revenue needs to be greater than your expenses.

Some expenses will be "fixed" because they do not change month to month. An example might be rent. If your office space rent is $3,000 per month, you must still pay $3,000 per month regardless of whether or not you have made any sales or earned any income.

Other type of expenses is a variable one. In the economic and budgeting world this is known as a variable "cost." This is a cost that increases with the level of sales or income. They are variable because the more income you generate, the greater costs you incur. The sales commissions expense is an example of a variable expense—the greater the sales revenue, the greater the sales commission. You may want to do research before starting your business to determine what comprises your fixed and variable costs. Certain types of businesses have an established profit margin. This information may be available by simply asking other professionals in your field. Your accountant has generally seen thousands and thousands of tax returns and may be able to give you an idea of the average "cost of sales" or "profit margins" for your particular business. The averages for certain industries are also compiled by financial ratings organizations such as Dun & Bradstreet, Moody's, and Standard & Poor's. For example, if you were starting a retail sales/coffee house, you could compare your sales, gross profit ratio, and net income to the averages for the retail sales/coffee industry compiled by Dun & Bradstreet.

One new business started their budget by jotting down all projected costs—right down to the mileage costs to get to their prospective clients. Then they decided to "get real" about the way things really worked. They trimmed these same projected expenses by 25%. The owners decided they would have to test their willpower and run a "tight ship." They were also one of the few businesses in California to increase their bottom line profit in the recession years and ultimately sell their business to a *Fortune* 500 company. Their advice is simple: *"Watch the bottom line and your budget. There is no reason to get greedy or spend your earnings all in the beginning, or there may not be anything left at the end."*

FOLLOW-UP IS THE KEY TO SUCCESS

When you compare your anticipated revenue and costs to the actual amounts, you will notice some variances. Your first managerial task is to determine whether these variances are normal. An increase in the utility companies' fees would naturally increase your annual costs for utilities. A look at your actual advertising costs might show that you are way over budget. Perhaps this is because of the extra advertising you decided to run. The managerial question is, "Did it pay off?" Keep in mind that you are the boss, and you are the only one who can make the budget process work.

There are certain signals to keep in mind when running your business. These will tell you that you are not charging enough, your overhead is too high, or you don't have a market that will support your business. If you begin to have problems paying your payroll taxes, you need to seek professional advice immediately. Another bad signal is using your credit cards to finance your cash shortage and then not having the ability to pay them in full. If these things start to happen, you should reassess your situation before it is too late. Take some advice from your

Certified Public Accountant. They have seen these situations often and will be able to give you some assistance in analyzing your financial information.

YOUR BUDGET

Many accounting books will tell you that the starting point in preparing a master budget is setting up a sales forecast and working towards the bottom line. As a small business owner, you may need to develop a reverse budget (i.e., one that is generated by your expenses rather than projected sales). This is typically what the government does. It develops the budget based on costs. Unlike the government, however, you must cut costs if you do not meet the necessary revenue goals.

The example at the end of this chapter is an over-simplified cash budget which focuses merely on the cash flow necessary to cover costs. This chapter does not deal with the added complexities of inventory issues or debt financing that your business might have. The calculation of the related tax liability has also been over-simplified. Again these are the areas which require the use of your local Certified Public Accountant. Study the example at the end of this chapter and try to work through your own budget. If you can't cover your overhead costs in your first draft, try streamlining your fixed costs. This is usually the area where most businesses spend needlessly. Then ask yourself whether or not you can create a sales level to cover these costs. If not, you should ask yourself if you really have a customer base or market that can adequately support your business. At a minimum, you should compare your revenue and expenses to your budget on a quarterly basis in order to keep track of the financial pulse of your business.

OTHER ITEMS TO ANALYZE
YOUR BUSINESS

There are other tools you can use to analysis the performance of your business, such as ratios. A ratio expresses the mathematical relationship between one quantity and another. This is expressed in terms of a percentage or rate. Many accounting and software programs will generate financial ratios as routine output.

You will now see the significant contribution your accounting information makes to your management process. A summary of various ratios and formulas follows this chapter. However, your primary financial statements can be analyzed using the liquidity ratios, the profitability ratios, or solvency ratios as described below:

The liquidity ratio measures your ability to pay your debts and to meet unexpected needs for cash. Several types of liquidity ratios include the *"current ratio,"* the *"acid-test ratio,"* *"receivables turnover,"* and *"inventory turnover."*

The profitability ratio measures the operating success of your business. Several types of profitability ratios include the *"profit margin ratio"* (return of sales), the *"asset turnover ratio,"* the *"return on assets ratio,"* and the *"price-earnings ratio."*

The solvency ratio measures the ability of your business to survive over a long period of time. Several types of solvency ratios include the *"debt to total assets ratio"* and the *"times interest earned ratio."*

The liquidity ratios are the ones most likely to impact your business:

1. *The "acid-test ratio"* $= \dfrac{\text{cash} + \text{marketable securities} + \text{receivable}}{\text{all current liabilities}}$
(debts due within one year)

The acceptable average for most industries is 1:1 which tells you that you have one dollar of liquid assets for every dollar of current debt. You will notice that this does not include your inventory which may not be readily saleable. If your current assets are $80,000 and your current liabilities are $90,000, then your ratio is as follows:

$$\frac{\$80,000}{\$90,000} = .89$$

This means that for every 0.89 cents of assets, your company has $1 of debt. Obviously, a ratio of 1:1 is more healthy. A ratio of 2:1 is even better.

2. *The "receivables turnover ratio"* $= \dfrac{\text{net credit sales}}{\text{average net receivables}}$

This measures how quickly your receivables can be converted to cash. To get an average of net receivables, use the receivables at the beginning of your year ($50,000) and the receivables at the end of your year ($62,000). Add them together and divide by two to get the "average."

Beginning $50,000 + Ending $62,000 = $112,000 ÷ 2 = $56,000 as "average receivables."

Assume your total credit sales are $560,000. Your accounts receivable turnover is 10.00 times, calculated as follows:

$$\frac{\text{net credit sale } \$560,000}{\text{average net receivables } \$56,000} = 10.00 \text{ times}$$

To determine your average collection period, divide your turnover ratio of 10.00 times into 365 days to obtain 36.5 days. This means that the average collection period for your receivables is 36.5 days or approximately every five weeks. You should use this ratio to evaluate your credit and collection policies. The general rule is that the collection period should not greatly exceed the time allowed for payment. Keep in mind that the more delinquent your receivables become, the harder they are to collect. Once they are passed 180 days, they become also impossible to collect.

3. *The "inventory turnover ratio"* $= \dfrac{\text{cost of goods sold}}{\text{average inventory}}$

This ratio measures the number of times your inventory is sold during the year. You can obtain your average inventory in the same method in which you determined average receivables. Beginning of year, plus end of year, divided by two. These inventory figures should show up on your balance sheet at the beginning and end of the year. The "cost of goods sold" figure will be obtained from your income statement.

For example: $$\frac{\text{cost of goods sold } \$47{,}000}{\text{average inventory } \$9{,}400} = 5.00 \text{ times}$$

This means that your inventory has "turned over" five times during the year. Generally, the faster the inventory turnover, the less cash is tied up in inventory and the less chance of obsolescence. Now divide 365 days by 5 times and you know that it takes you an average of 73 days to sell your inventory. Keep in mind that inventory turnover ratios vary among industries. A grocery store chain typically has a turnover of 10 times while a jewelry store only has an average turnover of 1.3 times.

It is important to note that the usefulness of the budgetary process and the analytical ratios is limited by the use of estimates and the application of alternative accounting methods. You may price your inventory with *"First-cost-In is the First-cost-Out"* (FIFO) or the *"Last-cost-In is the First-cost-Out"* (LIFO). There are also a large number of ratios which cannot be practically covered in this text. However, the key to success is getting good control of your accounting process, using the information for management decision making, and listening to the advice of your professional consultants.

CREATING YOUR OWN BUDGET

Annual Fixed Expenses	Example	Your Business
Rent ($500 × 12)	$ 6,000	_____
Phone ($100 × 12)	1,200	_____
Utilities ($100 × 12)	1,200	_____
Office Supplies ($50 × 12)	600	_____
Equipment Rent or Lease ($375 × 12)	4,500	_____
Wages (if you have employees)	15,000	_____
Payroll Taxes (approx. 10% of wages)	1,500	_____
Worker's Compensation Insurance	250	_____
Health Insurance ($100 × 12)	600	_____
Liability Insurance ($100 × 12)	600	_____
Disability Insurance ($300 pr yr.)	300	_____
Professional Licenses ($300 pr yr.)	300	_____
Dues/Subscriptions ($25 × 12)	300	_____
Your take home pay ($1000 × 12)	12,000	_____
Federal and State Taxes on the take-home pay (consult your tax advisor) ($1000 × 40% × 12)	4,800	_____
TOTAL FIXED EXPENSES	**$49,150**	

Variable Costs

This is when you need to know the relationship of the cost of your product to the sales price. This is determined from all of your hard research, consulting with other professionals in your field, or asking your accountant.

Shipping/Freight (2% of sales price)
Product Cost (33% of sales price)
Other Materials/Supplies (5% of sales price)
Commissions (12% of sales price)

Total variable sales (50% of sales price)

Sales Level

Based on the amount of funds the sample business would need to pay the variable costs and the fixed costs, you can now determine the sales level. Remember, sales less cost of sales (50%) = 50% remaining to cover fixed costs. Use the following formula:

Sales of X — less variable costs 50% X =	$49,150	Fixed costs
100% X — less 50% X =	$49,150	
50% X =	$49,150	
50% X =	$49,150	
50%	50%	
X (Sales) =	$98,300	

After working through the math, you can see that your income in terms of sales must be $98,300 per year. If you cannot reasonably expect this level of income, you should reassess your overhead expenses, or the whole idea of going into business for yourself.

Ratio	Formula	Purpose or Use
Liquidity Ratios		
1. Current ratio	Current assets / Current liabilities	Measures short-term debt-paying ability
2. Acid-test or quick ratio	Cash + marketable securities + receivable (net) / Current liabilities	Measure immediate short-term liquidity
3. Receivables turnover	Net credit sales / Average net receivable	Measures liquidity of receivables
4. Inventory turnover	Cost of goods sold / Average inventory	Measures liquidity of inventory
Profitability Ratios		
5. Profit margin	Net income / Net sales	Measures net income generated by each dollar of sales

6. Asset turnover	$\dfrac{\text{Net sales}}{\text{Average assets}}$	Measures how efficiently assets are used to generate sales
7. Return on assets	$\dfrac{\text{Net Income}}{\text{Average assets}}$	Measures overall profitability of assets used
8. Return on common stockholders' equity	$\dfrac{\text{Net income}}{\text{Average common stockholders' equity}}$	Measures profitability of owner's investment
9. Earnings per share	$\dfrac{\text{Net income}}{\text{Weighted average common shares outstanding}}$	Measures net income earned on each share of common stock
10. Price-earnings ratio	$\dfrac{\text{Market price per share of stock}}{\text{Earnings per share}}$	Measures the ratio of the market price per share to earnings per share
11. Payout ratio	$\dfrac{\text{Cash dividends}}{\text{Net income}}$	Measures percentage of earnings distributed in the form of cash dividends

Solvency Ratios

12. Debt to total assets	$\dfrac{\text{Total debt}}{\text{Total assets}}$	Measures the percentage of total assets provided by creditors
13. Times interest earned	$\dfrac{\text{Income before income taxes and interest expense}}{\text{Interest expense}}$	Measures ability to meet interest payments as they come due

Checklist of Items for Starting a New Business

Read this book in its entirety. If you still want to open your own business, read through this checklist.

You should not make any purchases, sign any leases, or meet with an attorney or accountant until you have worked through Steps #1–11 regarding the budgeting and determined whether or not you have the appropriate financial resources to open a new business. Check off each step as you complete it.

You will need to work through Step #12 in order to determine whether or not you can break even on a monthly basis.

If you clear these hurdles, you are ready to start on the other things you will need to start your business.

1. Figure out your personal expenses and the amount of monthly take-home pay you need. Make sure not to duplicate insurances or other expenses which might be paid out of the business. _____

2. Take care of yourself before you leap into the new world of self-employment. _____

Take a vacation before you start. Do health things like doctor and dentist visits, especially while on someone else's health insurance. Enlist the support of family and friends. You can use this fan club for moral support. They will also be more understanding when you suddenly drop out of circulation. _____

Develop a physical outlet for stress: health club, moon walking, etc. The stress of being a business owner is much greater than you may think.   _____

3. Write down the nature of the product or services you will provide.   _____

4. Decide on a business form. Do some research about obtaining an attorney or CPA. Ask your friends or other business people. You want to make sure that both the attorney and CPA specialize in setting up businesses. Not all do.   _____

Find out about the related legal fees to set up a corporation or partnership.   _____

Find out about initial consulting fees from your accountant and costs related to tax preparation.   _____

5. Determine whether or not you will need employees. Write out a rough draft of their job description and the number of hours they will be working. Determine whether or not they will need any special skills or licenses.   _____

Determine their hourly rate or salary to arrive at monthly payroll costs. Figure an additional 10% expense for the employer portion of payroll taxes.   _____

6. Determine how much office space you will need and where it will be located. Look at office space in a similar area and try to get an idea of the cost per square foot. This will give you an idea of your monthly rental expense.   _____

Will you be renting an empty shell or an existing office? Are any modifications needed? If yes, you may need to retain the services of an architect who can design the construction plans and drawings for you. These fees are in addition to the construction costs.   _____

Try to get a rough idea on the cost of a build out. There are a variety of people who may have a rough idea, such as the architect, a landlord, a similar or neighboring business, and the construction estimator.   _____

If you are purchasing a franchise, you will usually be given an estimate.   _____

7. Determine the type of insurance to be carried and obtain quotes from selected agents/carriers. If it appears that the agent will not give you any information unless you buy something, ask for the advice of people in similar professions. _____

    malpractice _____

    worker's compensation _____

    life _____

    health _____

    disability _____

    fidelity bond for employees handling cash _____

    general liability _____

    office contents _____

    umbrella _____

    other (such as professional liability, error and omissions) _____

8. Determine whether or not you need a specialized telephone system or answering service. If an answering service, call around and get quotes for monthly service. If you need to make an equipment purchase, get an idea of the dollar amounts involved. Compare purchase vs. a lease. _____

Determine how many regular phone lines, fax lines, or modem lines you will need. Find out about the cost of installation. The cost of the phones and fax should be included in your fixed asset list in Step #10. _____

9. Determine whether or not you will be using a computer. _____

Make a decision on what type of software programs you will need (to include an accounting program). You should look at your software first—and buy the computer hardware that will accommodate it. Otherwise you might get a computer that won't run your programs. _____

List your software costs as well as your hardware costs. _____

Determine whether or not you will need to go "on line" or set up marketing through a World Wide Web. Find out about the related costs. _____

Don't buy anything until you have discussed your
accounting needs with your CPA and your computer
needs with a consultant. _____

Identify whether or not you will need the assistance of
someone to help your purchase, install and set up your
computer programs. Ask them about their set-up fees. _____

10. Make a detailed list of all other fixed assets needed to
run your business. List out the cost of the items if you
would have to purchase them new. Determine if you can
save money by buying any of the items used. _____

Make a list of locations or sources that will sell you the
assets you need. Some auctions accept cash only so ask
about this up front. _____

If some of the assets are financed by the manufacturer,
such as copiers, find out what the monthly lease terms are
to include the monthly dollar amount, and total number of
months. Don't forget to ask about the buy out at the end
of the lease. Are you going to need a large sum of cash
to buy back the asset? Or merely $1.00? _____

If you need to lease from a manufacturer, determine
whether or not you can obtain a bank or credit union
loan. The interest rate is usually much lower than that of
the manufacturer. _____

11. Draft out a marketing plan which includes a description of
your market, how you will access it, and the related
graphics or advertising costs. _____

Determine if you will have any one-time grand opening
costs. You may need to get quotes regarding the rental of
party tents, catering, and hot air balloons. _____

Determine the amount of monthly advertising you would
like to do and where/how it should be done. _____

Find out what you need to do to get listed in the white
and yellow pages. _____

Determine whether or not you will join your local Chamber
of Commerce or other professional organizations. What
are their monthly or annual dues? _____

12. Estimate your start-up cash needs to determine whether or not you will need financing. _____

Figure your start-up expenses: _____

    Step #4   legal and accounting costs _____

    Step #6   lease build out if any _____

    Step #8   phone installation costs _____

    Step #9   computer software costs _____

    Step #9   computer hardware costs _____

    Step #9   on line or World Wide Web costs _____

    Step #9   computer consultant fees _____

    Step #10   costs of other fixed assets _____

    Step #11   grand opening costs _____

Add up the total for start-up expenses: _____

If you do not have the cash resources to pay for these costs, you will need to obtain a loan. Visit with local bankers and ask about their loan programs. Many of them will refer you to an agency that assists with federal government loans such as the Small Business Administration (SBA). _____

Determine whether or not you can qualify for a loan. Begin the loan application process. _____

Also ask your bank about business credit cards. _____

13. If you do not need a loan, or the loan goes through, you will need to figure out your monthly cash needs for **each month of your first year in business.** _____

Figure out your monthly expenses:

    Step #5   wage expenses _____

    Step #6   monthly rent _____

    Step #7   insurance amounts _____

    Step #8   monthly answering service _____

    Step #8   phone system lease payment _____

    Step #10 monthly lease costs of assets not purchased _____

    Step #11 monthly advertising/promotion costs _____

    Step #11 Chamber of Commerce and other dues _____

Figure in other overhead items: _____

   estimated monthly phone bill   _____

   estimated office supplies   _____

   estimated bank/credit charges   _____

   estimated bookkeeping fees   _____

   your draw from the business (refers back to Step #2)   _____

   the amount needed for the loan repayment   _____

Estimate your monthly income: _____

   Write down how you came to this figure   _____

   For example: three installations per day at 1 hr each @ \$55 per hour = \$165 per day. Figure 20 work days per month = \$3,300 monthly income.

   For example: 80 customers per day, spending an average of \$5.00 per sale = \$400 per day. Figure 24 work days per month (open on Saturday) = \$9,600 monthly income.

Determine whether or not your monthly income will cover your monthly expenses. If not, do not proceed, do not pass go, do not collect \$200. Once you have determined your monthly income and expenses, assume a real life scenario—reduce your income by 25%.   _____

Determine whether or not you can cut costs enough to make it.   _____

If you can, congratulations, you are on your way to starting a new business.   _____

14. Now that the financing is in place, and you have determined your income will cover your expenses and result in a net profit, re-read Chapter 3 and try to set up your chart of accounts. Meet with an accountant and have her/him review your software and computer needs. Your CPA may save you some research time by recommending an accounting program.   _____

Write a draft of your accounting system and review it with your CPA. You should review the following: _____

   Your billing and accounts receivable system   _____

Your cash disbursements system   _____

Your payroll system   _____

Make sure to re-read the issues discussed in Chapter 5—
inventory, cash vs. accrual, year end, and determine
whether or not these apply to your business.   _____

15. Make the appointment with your attorney and set up the
legal framework. In some cases, the attorney will need the
opening balance sheet from the accountant before any
legal work can be done.   _____

16. Re-read Chapter 2 and obtain all related ID numbers,
sales tax numbers, city/county licenses. Use the checklist
at the back of the chapter.   _____

17. Once you have your ID numbers, you can open your
business checking account.   _____

Order a check endorsement stamp "FOR DEPOSIT ONLY"
for your business account.   _____

*[At this point, you have your financing, your legal
framework, your tax identification number and checking
account. The sequence of the following steps can be
rearranged depending upon your particular situation.]*

18. Locate office space and negotiate terms. Finalize build-
out if necessary. Coordinate with construction crew if
applicable. Determine your "opening date."   _____

19. Order the necessary furniture, equipment and phone
systems.   _____

20. Order your letterhead, business cards, and office forms.   _____

21. Have signs made for your office. Make sure to have all
appropriate OSHA signs and personnel posters ordered.   _____

22. Run an advertisement for employees. Obtain applications,
begin the interviews and hiring dates. Remember if they
are hired, you should set up a personnel file. Obtain Form
W-4 and Form I-9.   _____

23. Establish credit with various vendors (supplies, utilities,
etc.). This can be done with the information used to
obtain your bank loan.   _____

24. Determine your inventory levels and needs for office supplies. Order in advance so your items arrive before your first day. _____

25. Set up your computer and accounting program. Make an appointment with your accountant to visit your office and make sure your accounting program is ready for your first day. _____

26. Coordinate your grand opening party and advertising. _____

27. Make an appointment with yourself for a monthly check up on your business. _____

28. Make an appointment with your accountant for your first quarterly check up. This is a good time for fine tuning! _____

Good luck!

B

Resources and Publications

GOVERNMENT PUBLICATIONS AND RESOURCES

Publications

IRS Publication 15

IRS Notice 931, Deposit Requirements

Circular E, Employer's Tax Guide

IRS Publication 519, US Tax Guide for Aliens

IRS Publication 937, Employment Taxes and Information Returns

IRS Publication 1679, A Guide to Backup Withholding

The State Employment Development Department Employers' Guide

Resources

The IRS usually has FREE seminars on a monthly basis for new and potential business owners. They publish a quarterly schedule.

SCORE—The Service Core of Retired Executives offers a monthly workshop at many locations. This is a federal government office. You should check your local directory for your nearest SCORE office. There is usually a small fee (about $35).

C

Records Retention Schedule

	Retention Period
Accident reports/claims (settled cases)	7 years
Accounts payable ledgers and schedules	7 years
Accounts receivable ledgers and schedules	7 years
Audit reports	Permanently
Bank reconciliations	2 years
Bank statements	3 years
Capital stock and bond records: ledgers, transfer registers, stubs showing issues, record of interest coupons, options, etc.	Permanently
Cash books	Permanently
Charts of accounts	Permanently
Checks (canceled–see exception below)	7 years
Checks (canceled for important payments, i.e., taxes, purchases of property, special contracts, etc. Checks should be filed with the papers pertaining to the underlying transaction.)	Permanently
Contracts, mortgages, notes, and leases	
(expired)	7 years
(still in effect)	Permanently
Correspondence (general)	2 years
Correspondence (legal and important matters only)	Permanently
Correspondence (routine) with customers and/or vendors	2 years
Deeds, mortgages, and bills of sale	Permanently
Depreciation schedules	Permanently

	Retention Period
Duplicate deposit slips	2 years
Employment applications	3 years
Expense analyses/expense distribution schedules	7 years
Financial statements (year-end, other optional)	Permanently
Garnishments	7 years
General/private ledgers, year-end trial balance	Permanently
Insurance policies (expired)	3 years
Insurance records, current accident reports, claims, policies, etc.	Permanently
Internal audit reports (longer retention periods may be desirable)	3 years
Internal reports (miscellaneous)	3 years
Inventories of products, materials, and supplies	7 years
Invoices (to customers, from vendors)	7 years
Journals	Permanently
Magnetic tape and tab cards	1 year
Minute books of directors, stockholders, bylaws, and charter	Permanently
Notes receivable ledgers and schedules	7 years
Option records (expired)	7 years
Patents and related papers	Permanently
Payroll records and summaries	7 years
Personnel files (terminated)	7 years
Receiving sheets	1 year
Retirement and pension records	Permanently
Requisitions	1 year
Sales commission reports	3 years
Sales records	7 years
Scrap and salvage records (inventories, sales, etc.)	7 years
Stenographer's notebooks	1 year
Stock and bond certificates (canceled)	7 years
Stockroom withdrawal forms	1 year
Subsidiary ledgers	7 years
Tax returns and worksheets, revenue agents' reports, and other documents relating to determination of income tax liability	Permanently

	Retention Period
Time books/cards	7 years
Trademark registrations and copyrights	Permanently
Training manuals	Permanently
Union agreements	Permanently
Voucher register and schedules	7 years
Vouchers for payments to vendors, employees, etc. (includes allowances and reimbursement of employees, officers, etc., for travel and entertainment expenses)	7 years
Withholding tax statements	7 years

D

Glossary

Account   This is a term used to describe an individual accounting item and help organize a business. An "account" represents the various increases and decreases to a specific asset, liability or equity item of your business. Accounts are divided into eight categories (assets, liabilities, equity, income, cost of sales, expenses, other income, and other expenses).

Accountant   Extremely intelligent, logical thinker. Can't always coordinate the color of his or her clothes. Some are known to wear glasses, pencils behind their ears, and act like nerdy little gnomes.

Accounting equation   An ancient Babylonian theory that holds since each trade or each transaction is always equal, the financial records must always be equal. Assets = liabilities + owner's equity.

Accounts payable   An account which represents the amount owed to vendors for items or services.

Accounts receivable   An account which represents the amount your customers owe you for items or services received.

Accrual method of accounting   A method of accounting which recognizes revenue when earned (and not when the money is received). It recognizes expenses when incurred (i.e., when you become liable for a payment and not when you pay it).

Adjusting journal entry (AJE)   When analyzing your trial balance, any errors between the ending account balances and the actual amounts are corrected with an AJE. The entry is made after analyzing why there is a difference. The adjusting entry can then be (1) recorded in your general journal, (2) posted to your ledger, and ultimately (3) summarized on the new revised trial balance. This should be a standard part of your accounting process.

Assets   These are things or resources your business owns. The types of account may be "cash," "inventory," "furniture," "vehicles," etc.

Balance sheet   A name for a financial statement which provides a snapshot of a company's condition and contains the ending balances of a company's assets, liabilities, and equity accounts as of a certain date.

Bank statement A report issued by a financial institution which shows the activity of your cash account for a month to include a list of all of your deposits, and all of the checks which cleared.

Budget The expected future activity for a business. Usually based on past experience, budgets are useful for future planning and comparing actual performance with planned performance.

Capital asset Tangible resources that are used in the operations of a business and are not intended for resale to customers. They are also called plant and equipment or *"fixed assets."*

Cash basis of accounting A method of accounting in which sales are recorded when the money is received and not when the services are delivered. Expenses are recognized when paid, and not at the time they are incurred.

Cash disbursements Money paid out by a business, usually to vendors or refund checks to customers.

Cash flow A written listing of where the company's money came from and where it went for a specific period of time.

Cash receipts Money received by a company, usually taking the form of payments made by customers. Also referred to as "receipts."

Chart of accounts A list of all of the accounts in a company's ledger. This list is made up by the owner. The accounts are summarized in a systematic manner that represents the way they would show up on the financial statement.

Corporation A separate legal entity which exists under the authority granted by the Secretary of State. Has its own legal rights, responsible for its own debts, and pays its own taxes. Corporate income does not flow through to the individual. Typically, the owners or stockholders are protected from the liabilities of the business.

Cost of sales These are the direct costs related to the sale of merchandise or the performance of the service. These accounts might be "raw materials," "commissions," or "delivery expenses."

Credit A term that represents the right side of a column.

Debit A term that represents the left side of a column.

Depreciation Depreciation is the process of allocating the cost of an asset to an expense category based on its useful life. It adjusts for the wear and tear of fixed assets.

Estimated payments Additional payments of tax made to the federal and state governments on a quarterly basis. Estimated payments are made because the income earned is not subject to the withholding as seen in a W-2. These quarterly payments are based on the estimated earnings through the year.

Equity This is the difference between your assets and your liabilities. Types of equity accounts might be "common stock" or "proprietor's capital," "retained earnings" or "owner's equity."

Expense   These are the general operating expenses incurred to run your business. Expense "accounts" might include "rents," "telephone," "utilities," "office supplies," and "interest expense."

Federal employer identification number (EIN)   An identification number assigned to a business by the IRS for tax reporting purposes. This is required because your business becomes its own legal entity. This number can be obtained by filing a *"Form SS-4"* with the Internal Revenue Service.

Fiscal year   A tax year of twelve months which ends with a month other than December. For example, some city governments have fiscal years that run from 7/1/19X1 to 6/30/19X2.

Income   This is the money received from the sale of merchandise, the performance of a service, or the rental of property. Income accounts might be "merchandise sales" or "installation fees." It is also known as revenue. It usually carries a credit balance.

Income statement   A financial statement showing a company's performance over a period of time. Also referred to as a "Profit & Loss Statement."

Independent contractor   An independent contractor is a worker who is subject to "control" and "direction," but is not restricted as to the method of how the work should be done. A Form 1099 is issued at year end and sent to the IRS which reports the amount paid to the independent contractor.

Internal control   A company policy or plan that safeguards assets and enhances the accuracy and reliability of accounting records.

Inventory   Goods held for sale or resale in a manufacturing or merchandising business. It includes all finished goods, partly finished goods, and raw materials and supplies which have been acquired for resale.

Invoice   The written record of a sale.

Journal   A collection of information which records a business transaction in chronological order. It contains the *debit and credit* amounts for each transaction. A journal can be a sheet of paper, a notebook, or a computer file. Is known as the book of original entry. There are various types of journals such as the general journal, sales journal, purchases journal, inventory journal, cash receipts journal, and cash disbursements journal.

Journalizing   Recording entries to a journal.

Ledger   This is the book of second entry. It is a place to record the analytical activity for each account individually. For example, the ledger card for sales shows only the sales activity (i.e., only the credits). The equipment ledger card shows only the equipment. The ledger does not have to be an actual "card." It can be a sheet of paper or a computer file.

Liabilities   These are debts payable to others such as a bank loan payable, amounts payable to your vendors/creditors, amounts payable for sales taxes, or even amounts owed to your employees. Your accounts might be "bank loan payable" or "taxes payable."

Limited liability companies (LLCs) Hybrid business entities created by statute which combine certain characteristics of corporations with other characteristics associated with partnerships. LLCs are intended to provide limited liability to its owners, have the ability to hold property in its own name, and sue or be sued (similar to a corporation). LLCs, like partnerships, offer the advantages of one level of tax without the restrictions of an S-Corporation. LLCs permit non-pro rata distributions and special allocations of profits and losses.

Listed property Listed property is usually any property that lends itself to personal use. Generally it includes passenger automobiles weighing 6,000 pounds or less, motorcycles, pick-up trucks, photographic equipment, communication equipment, video recording equipment, cellular telephones, and computers.

Net income The total of all income accounts minus the sum of all expenses and costs of sales. It is also called Net Profit or "the bottom line."

Other expense These are costs or expenses that are not related to the sale of merchandise or the running of your business. This is reserved for the unusual and infrequent type of expense. An example might be "flood loss."

Other income This is revenue that is not part of your everyday income such as interest income or special one-time sale of assets. An example of this type of category might be "interest income."

Partnership Two or more individuals who have joined together to run a business enterprise. Can be a general or limited partnership. A partnership becomes its own legal entity. Rights and obligations of partners are detailed in partnership agreement.

Posting The process of transferring the information from a journal to a ledger.

Reconciling The process of verifying that the ending figure in any given account agrees with the backup documentation for the same accounts.

Retained earnings This is a term used by corporations. It represents the total earnings/equity throughout the corporation's lifetime, not including the current year.

S-Corporation Type of corporation that has special treatment. Basically it is a corporation in all aspects, except that the income is taxed similarly to that of a partnership, i.e., the various items of income, expense, and credits flow through to the individual stockholders.

Sole proprietorship A business owned and operated by one individual or a husband and wife team.

Trial balance A trial balance is a list of all of your accounts and their ending balances at a given time. This should usually be prepared at the end of each month, but it can be done at any time. The primary purpose of the trial balance is to prove the mathematical equality of the debts and credits after posting.

Wages Money paid to employees for work done, including salary or hourly earnings, bonuses, or commission. These are reported at year end on a Form W-2.

Year end The end of a business's financial year. For most sole proprietors, this will be December. If you are not a December year end, you are considered to have a "fiscal year."

Index